THE CORPORATE CULT
Surviving and Transforming Your Career

by Diane Kasunic, Ph.D.

11-27-00

Ann:

Best wishes in your career and all of life's challenges.

Diane Kasunic

ISBN #0-9679382-0-1

First Edition — May, 2000

Printed in the United States of America

For more information, write or email:
Hero Training
PO Box 1137
Birmingham, MI 48012-1137
DrDianeKasunic@home.com
foxythecat@aol.com

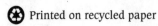 Printed on recycled paper

TABLE OF CONTENTS

DEDICATION

I dedicate this book to all of the employees of *Corporate America*. I hope that they can learn by my experience and enrich *Corporate America* by transforming their careers.

This book should be used as a motivational tool. It should help you reflect, and you should consider keeping a journal while you read the book. Each section contains real life stories, followed by a set of strategies. They reinforce each other.

As I come to a fuller appreciation of my own worth, I grow in confidence, in my sense of adequacy, and in my capability to live responsibly and effectively. This personal growth contributes to emotional spiritual warmth, which becomes part of my sense of myself and my relationship with others. Appreciating my own worth and importance is futile if it fails to foster responsible character and integrity in my actions. Character needs to be nurtured. It proceeds from a healthy sense of myself and, like any living entity, it needs to be nourished.

Toward a State of Esteem
California Task Force, January 1990

PREFACE

I never learned to ice skate. I had only been ice skating once, when I was about twenty-one. It was an unforgettable experience for me and the patient friend, Richard, who went with me. I had what seemed to be the weakest ankles on the planet. I could "stay up" for only a matter of seconds, literally. I was not sure why. I remember feeling scared and frustrated, but not really understanding, or wanting to understand what the problem or obstacle was. At the time, I guess I thought that the obstacle was the ice, or the skates, or my mood, or the people around me.

At the age of thirty-something, I decided to learn how to ice skate. An inner voice and an inexplicable drive compelled me. I made calls to several local ice arenas to get their hours. When I found one that was close by and had regular open skating, I decided to go and check it out. The next day I got into my car and drove for thirty minutes, looking for an arena. It was only about six miles from my house and in an area quite familiar to me. I drove for thirty minutes without finding a clue to lead me to this arena, although I believed that I knew where it was. I went home discouraged and frustrated, but was still determined.

I got on the phone and called the arena, asking for explicit instructions from my home. After I received the instructions, I got back into my car and drove to the ice arena. It was about 500 feet from where I had been driving on my first excursion.

I went inside and looked at the rink. There were about twenty people skating on the ice. It looked as if they were going so fast and were so confident of their strides that I began to cry. I was grossly intimidated by this drama occurring on the ice. I looked at the skaters through the Plexiglas doors and said to myself, "I can't do this." I will never learn to skate. Some people are just not cut out for it and I must be one of them." I knew that trying to get out there on the ice, on my own, would be a big disaster and a humiliating experience that I did not need. I inquired about lessons. It was so late in the year that lessons were over for the season. I was sad, disappointed but relieved, and I made the vow to myself that I would learn to skate when the next season opened.

Sure enough, the season came and I managed to procrastinate through October and most of November. My conscience got the best of me just before Thanksgiving and I asked my husband, Kevin, to go ice skating with me. Kevin is the type who is a natural athlete. Sports and sporting movements come easily to him. The good news for me is that he has a coach temperament. I felt that his patience and skill could bail me out of the humiliation, which I had avoided for so long. And so we went ice skating on a Saturday afternoon in November.

If you have never been ice skating and have any doubts about your ability to conquer this sport, I do not suggest that you follow my lead and try it on a Saturday afternoon in peak season. There were probably one hundred people there, although it seemed like a million, not to mention small children who had mastered the ice with total freedom and agility. These confident kids had a sense of self so strong, that they were oblivious to all other skaters. Others were seemingly invisible to them as they charged in any and all directions without hesitation or inhibition. Knowing that I had Kevin's hand to hold was a big crutch, which I "needed." While holding on to him, I was able to stand up without falling, which was a big improvement over my first excursion with Richard. We went the following Saturday and my brother-in-law, Tim, came with us. After a great deal of coaching, he and Kevin got a little bored with my first gear speed and felt that they were doing an excellent job of explaining how to skate. Why didn't I get it right? Couldn't I hear them?

I finally got angry and decided to sit and watch, freeing them to join the circuit. As I watched the skaters, many people came up to me and offered their advice and tips on movement for pushing off; lots and lots of suggestions. Most began by saying, "Is this your first time?" It was no longer my first time, so I felt a little guilty as I looked them in the eye and said, "Yes." The more unsolicited suggestions I received, the angrier I became.

Finally, a little girl, a very pretty little blonde, about five years old came up to me and said, "I can skate better than you can." I was enraged. I felt so ashamed of myself. A woman with all of my credentials and accomplishments could be upset by competition with a kindergartner. Luckily, I managed to get out an appropriate response and said, "Why yes you can, that's very good, honey." Looking back, I'll bet the "honey" had a bite on it.

After being "put into my place" by a child, I examined, why, why, why is it so hard, so seemingly impossible for me to do this sport. I looked at all of the people racing around and having fun. They were average people. There was nothing special about them except that they could ice skate and I could not. I realized that I was scared to ice skate. Scared. Huh! I was terrified and my legs became paralyzed with fear each time I tried. The more input I received, the harder it became and the more scared I felt. What would happen if they saw that I could not do what they suggested? What if they thought I was uncoordinated or stupid? And worst of all, WHAT IF I FELL? There was no way that I could handle that, not me. "I'm a winner. I don't fall!" Well, I certainly was not going to fall from the comfortable bench, on which I sat and moped.

When Kevin and Tim were done skating and asked me to try it again on my own, I tried to explain how scared I was of falling. I received very little empathy. It became very clear to me that in order to ice skate; I had to get rid of my fear of the ice and falling. I had to free myself of any inhibitions that I had been carrying around.

Kevin and I went back for about three more consecutive Saturdays and I continued my pretend skating routine, practically cemented to his arm. I am sure that I almost cut off his circulation. He was patient and entertained my helpless fright until I no longer could bear the thought of going ice skating with this victim posture. People were starting to recognize me. I was afraid they would notice no or little improvement. People were still making comments and giving unsolicited advice. One man started skating backward in front of me and said, "Oh, come on and smile already, it ain't so bad." These comments only made me more self-conscious. I discovered that the Siamese twin posture that I imposed upon my husband only made me feel inferior, repressed, disabled, incompetent and dependent. What a mistake! When I accepted this reality, I was determined to transform myself into an able, competent and independent skater. I felt like a disgrace, not to be able to go on the ice unless I was holding my husband's hand, even though God blessed me with very healthy limbs. This was a disgrace, or so I felt.

I called the ice arena and inquired about lessons. They explained that they held two sets of classes. Although I was technically available for either set, I convinced myself that they were at inconvenient times. I stopped thinking about skating for a few weeks. A month later, I again called the arena inquiring about a private lesson. I scheduled one. I knew that I was too frightened to learn this sport in front of a group. I wanted as much privacy as possible; in fact I asked the instructor if I could rent the arena for myself during the lesson. Of course she said no and informed me that there would only be a few people on the ice at that time.

Four and one-half months after my initial November experience, I was skating on my own during the week and in crowds on the weekends. My husband bought me a pair of skates, which solidified my commitment to the ice. This occurred after only two brief lessons. I am still no Olympic gold medal winner, but I learned how to ice skate and became a roller blader as well. Both are like flying. I mean so literally and metaphorically. What I found was that skating is so much like life. For the best results, skating should be handled just as one should handle his or her career in order to survive and grow.

1. Hold your head up and gaze forward.

2. Keep a straight posture and favor a lean toward the future.

3. Never look back.

4. Go at your own speed.

5. Don't pay much attention to unsolicited feedback.

6. Don't look at people who fall, because you will lose your balance; energy is catchy.

7. Don't tighten up your body. Stay relaxed and flexible. Bend your knees slightly to ensure flexibility, increased speed and balance.

8. Before you start, make sure that you have considered falling as a contingency. Practice falling and make sure you know how to do it safely. At least know how you will get up. Act out your strategy to get up. Sit on the ice and when you know that you will have no trouble getting up, you will not be afraid to fall. Because you will not be afraid to fall, you will not fall.

Breathe deeply. Be conscious of your breath. So often like life and especially in any situation the least bit uncomfortable or new, we forget to breathe. Breathing is the most fundamental and primitive source of life and energy. By not breathing, we commit self-sabotage. Go at your own speed...again!

NOW ASK YOURSELF:

- HAS YOUR CAREER CAUSED YOU TO LOSE YOUR BREATH?

- HAS YOUR CAREER CAUSED YOU TO LOSE YOUR BALANCE?

- DO YOU FIND YOURSELF VOID OF A FORWARD GAZE AND A HIGHLY HELD HEAD?

- DO YOU HAVE A VICE GRIP ON YOUR EGO?

- ARE YOU SETTING YOUR TIMER AT SOMEBODY ELSE'S SPEED?

- ARE YOU AFRAID OF FALLING, OR WORSE YET, DO YOU DENY THE POSSIBILITY OF FALLING?

- DO YOU KNOW HOW TO GET BACK UP?

- ARE YOU SCARED?

- HAS YOUR CAREER CAUSED YOU OR ASSISTED YOU TO LOSE YOUR FLEXIBILITY?

- IS YOUR CAREER ACCOMMODATING OR FACILITATING FEEBLE POSTURE?

- IS YOUR CAREER EMPOWERING YOUR DEEPEST FEARS OF INADEQUACY?

- DO YOU RECEIVE AND LISTEN TO EXCESSIVE UNSOLICITED FEEDBACK ABOUT YOUR STYLE?

- DOES YOUR ORGANIZATION'S CLIMATE ENCOURAGE YOU TO CONFORM?

If you answered YES or MAYBE to even one of these questions, you may have joined the *CORPORATE CULT*.

INTRODUCTION

Piaget singled out the adult's coercive or autocratic attitudes toward the child as a cause for his persistent subservience in educational codes and situations. Consequently, those exposed to them—for example, patients—are subjected to pressures to adapt by assuming the required postures of helplessness. *This leads to behavior judged appropriate or 'normal' within the system, but not necessarily outside of it. Resistance to the rules may be tolerated to varying degrees in different systems, but in any event tends to bring the individual into conflict with the group. Hence, most persons seek to conform rather than to rebel. Others try to adapt by becoming aware of the rules and of their limited, situation relevancy; this may make it possible to get along in the system, while also allowing the actor to maintain a measure of inner freedom.*

Thomas S. Szasz, M.D., *The Myth of Mental Illness*

The Corporate Cult Can Be Defined As Follows:

An informally organized culture within *Corporate America* with a separate code of rules and ethics, including many of the following:

- Discrimination
- Favoritism
- Intimidation as a source of motivation
- Politicking
- Decisions based on bias rather than fact
- Conformity
- Perfectionism standards, employed for the purpose of manipulation

There is often a separate code of rules and ethics, **void of** . . .

- Self-esteem
- Mutual respect
- Honest feedback which allows responses and fact finding
- Open adult communication
- Growth-producing norms
- Open-mindedness
- Fun or humor, not targeted as mockery

Images of the Corporate Cult

The drawing on the following page represents a look at the *Corporate Cult*. At first glance and even after further inspection, this sketch may look like a cursory or childlike drawing. In fact, this sketch contains mounds of reality, truth, and symbolism. We have all heard people use the phrase, "Have you no sense?" Unfortunately, this commonly used accusation is most typically

deciphered as meaning, "Have you no judgment, no mind, no logic, no brain or no conformity."

Somehow, we have managed to shift the focus of the word "sense" to have very intellectual or analytical connotation, and, of course, it certainly can. However, doesn't the word "senses" really have more to do with perception, sensation, consciousness, and understanding? I think so. Doesn't this word really refer to our centers for hearing, seeing, tasting, touching and smelling: situations that allow us to form intuitive suggestions? Primitive man was given these "senses" to survive, and they are still with us for the same reason. Why do we so quickly and easily bequeath them? By doing so, we surrender our power and creativity.

This socialization began in early childhood. A good example would be the commonly found puzzles for children. Many parents use them with their children. My parents got them for me and I could rarely see what was wrong with the picture. The kind of puzzles to which I am referring ask the child to find what is "wrong" with the picture. They may show an elephant carrying an umbrella or a bird using a computer and these would be defined as "wrong." I defined "wrong" differently than society at large. I still do. What is labeled as wrong in these pictures, I saw in my imagination and visualized through my creative energy. This is one of the reasons I love Santa Fe, New Mexico. This city has St. Francis of Assisi, the animal lover and friend, as a guardian. In Santa Fe there is an abundance of animal art, portraying animals doing unconventional deeds. You may see a zebra or giraffe filling in for Rudolph as Santa's guide or an elephant playing hopscotch.

In nursery schools there are bright colors, pictures of animals and flowers, creative images floating from the ceiling and soft fuzzy toys to handle. As we move through the years the classroom becomes more and more sterile and hard.

Finally, in the corporate world, we find an atmosphere largely void of stimuli that would provoke comfort, creativity, and security. We hear of stories about people bringing their pets or children to work. This remains the exception to the rule.

This process continues full cycle. The contrast between nursery school and nursing home is hard to compare. Largely, we tend to let our seniors live out their lives in the sterility of the corporate environment, leaving long behind the creative comforts that the soul appreciated in nursery school, which has the goal of developing and nurturing creativity and senses. Is this done only so life can become dull and desensitized?

The corporate employees in the sketch have truly lost their senses and would rule out the giraffe guiding Santa's sleigh. They are programmed as to what they will hear, what they want to hear, what they see, what they say, what they believe, and yes, what they actually taste and smell. Some are more, far-gone relative to others. Some still have their senses and are unhappy. Some have lost their vision and have no eyes, some have lost their rhythm, and they have no balance or drummer. Most are just ready to drink the flavor-of-the-month fruit punch, and I do mean punch.

People become desensitized. Some cannot smell. This means that they have lost their scent or identity. Through our sense of smell, our nose, we discover our scent. Animals do this all the time.

In Chinese medicine, the nose frequently represents the identity or self. Some believe that if one is experiencing nasal problems, then there is a possibility of an identity conflict of sorts. If breathing patterns are disrupted, it can mean that one cannot fully "take in" the breath or the situation.

There are few employees in the picture who have their senses and sense of self. Those are the employees who are

surviving and transforming their jobs in *Corporate America*.
Let's talk about how this can be done.

There is no longer a place in Corporate America for injustice and
ignorance which feed the senseless pawns who operate the Corporate Cult.

A Former Corporate Executive

I SAY: BE BRAVE! ENGAGE IN A TAKE-OVER. TAKE OVER
YOUR MIND AND SOUL! TAKE OVER YOUR CAREER!

Unrealistic Standards

In his book, *When I Say No, I Feel Guilty*, Manuel J. Smith,
Ph.D., discusses the assertive right of making mistakes. He says,
"You have the right to make mistakes—and be responsible for
them." He describes the manipulative logic which dysfunctional
systems use to tell us that we cannot make mistakes. You must
not make errors. Errors are wrong and cause problems to other
people. If you make errors, you should feel guilty. You are likely
to make more errors and problems and therefore you cannot cope
properly or make proper decisions. Other people should control
your behavior and decisions so you will not cause problems; in
this way you can make up for the wrong you have done to them.

The *Corporate Cult* is clearly a client of this system and
allegedly strives for perfection, only when this strategy can be
used to manipulate an employee. Even though innovative
constructs and consultants have forged ahead with positive
paradigms, the cult takes over. They talk it, but don't walk it.

Healthy working systems strive for improvement, growth, and healthy risk taking. They focus on the positive results.

I was an advocate of perfection until one day it became clear to me that it was erroneous. I sat gazing at a table on which two vases were placed. One vase contained a bunch of real roses. The second vase contained a bunch of plastic roses. The plastic roses were clearly perfect. They were flawless and because they were flawless, they did not look real. They looked fake and cheap. The real roses were not perfect; they had imperfections. When I pointed this out to the friend whom I was with, he replied, "What do you mean, they are perfect, each one is perfect." I then realized that perhaps my friend had a healthier interpretation of the word perfection than I. He was able to see the overall beauty and not the individual flaws of each particular rose. Although I noticed the flaws, I never once thought that the artificial flowers looked lovelier, more tender, more gentle or more real. Isn't this what it is all about, being real? Finding and accepting reality is a key to our survival. From now on, whenever I feel that I have lost my balance or perspective on the human condition, I go to the florist and look at the flowers, both synthetic and real.

The same analogy holds true for natural apples versus those treated with pesticides. The treated apples may be somewhat toxic or unnatural, but they look perfectly beautiful, whereas the natural or organic apples are often smaller and less shiny with visible flaws. The contrast can be quite dramatic. Which would you prefer to eat or feed to your child? Have we all been fed an unrealistic dosage of perfection? Our drive for perfection has stilted reality. The human condition is flawed and that is what makes it real and perfect. There is no such thing as a human without flaws. There are simply humans and then there is God. A balanced perspective and self-appreciation can help us adjust our view.

I want to be clear that although I am a new millennium woman and consider myself liberated and pro-women, in this book, the issues do not evolve around men womanizing the female gender. This is a reality and does occur only too often, but there are plenty of women who victimize and plenty of men who are victims. This goes for all races and creeds, as well. This book is about breaking away from the cult in a healthy and safe way, without losing your job. This book is about transforming your career and workplace so that you can be who you are, whether you are man, woman, gay, lesbian, Catholic, Buddhist, Jewish, Protestant, Hindu, a mom, a little league coach, a scoutmaster, shaman or whoever.

Cult Behaviors

There is a fundamental difference between playing the role or behaving a certain way versus becoming the role and adopting cult behaviors as your own. There is a fundamental difference between seeing options in a corporate problem-solving session, knowing that only one of them is "correct" or in the best interest of the stakeholders, versus realizing several options and knowing that only one of them is correct because of the cult's political acceptance. Unfortunately, in a *Corporate Cult*, where the environment is closed, those who leave their minds open to the greater good often leave themselves open. Predetermination is a reoccurring theme in the *Corporate Cult*. Things are already decided. The political agenda is in place. This can be especially frustrating for those who see what is happening and understand that the cult expects all involved to filter their responses according to cult norms. This way they can behave and respond appropriately, without dissension or challenge.

There are also times in which the actual behaviors of the cult become overtly offensive to others, offensive to the environment, and illegal or unethical; a word which I think is too unfamiliar to corporate discussions these days. These are the really tough situations and cause conflict and excess stress in many who have a conscience, and are conscious.

Many corporate behaviors provide a great deal of discomfort and take one away from his or her center of self. As you read the examples, you will most certainly acknowledge that these behaviors are not necessarily exclusive to the corporate environment. They tend to exist along with other superfluous pomp and circumstance.

Make Positive Choices

- Do volunteer work.
- Adopt a pet from a shelter.
- Perform random acts of kindness.
- Honor the environment.
- Smile at someone who looks as if they need it.
- Let someone into traffic on the race home.
- Say hello to seniors with a gleam and eye contact.
- Pray for someone you haven't seen for a while.
- Ask God to bless your enemies.
- Request that all you do be blessed and guided by Divinity.

CHAPTER ONE

Common and Curious
Phenomenon and Dysfunctions
Is It Like This Where You Work?

Elevators

I remember countless elevator trips on which I was alone with a group of "officers" or "higher levels." Did you ever notice that when they are in a gang, they frequently choose to refrain from conversation with employees who are of the ranks? This caste system tradition I found to be amazingly embarrassing for them. One might think that they feel their presence is so important they cannot be disturbed by one of a lesser pay scale or that perhaps by communicating with a "lower level," they would be displaying a character flaw. Perhaps they simply feel awkward or maybe this is simply indicative of our society's value system.

Overtime

Have you ever been efficient or organized enough to be able to come into work on time and leave on time, yet get the distinct feeling or perhaps even a warning that it is really not acceptable to leave work "on time?" The hours of nine to five actually mean from eight to six or probably a lot longer with weekend duty for promotional candidates. There are certainly periods in which overtime is necessary and mandatory and that comes with the package of being a professional, but what about if you really are through with your work? What if you are so competent that you get it all done, or would rather leave at 5:00 p.m. and work at home or work through lunch? The cult frequently expects members to stay after hours for no apparent reason. It is part of cult courting. This quasi logic involves proving your devotion to the cult as the number one priority in your life. This has caused problems for women who need to pick up children from day care, employees who have responsibility for an elderly family member, or fathers who coach Little League. These concerns have been brought to the attention of our political leaders and much legislation is currently pending regarding these issues.

I remember feeling the need to sneak out of work at 5:15 p.m. or 5:30 p.m., sometimes even 6:00 p.m. and later. I remember being challenged by peers that I was not devoted, had a light workload, or just didn't care. I remember going into the office on weekends and staying long after my work was completed and organized, praying that I would be seen by an "upper level" who could validate my strong sense of duty.

Teams and Meetings

Teams and team projects have become very popular. They can entail verbose meetings filled with pontificating and unorganized chaotic work plans. I have encountered many managers who work on teams and very much dislike it. Frequently, those attempting to provide organization are labeled as non-team players. Organization can threaten a team's togetherness. In his book, *People of the Lie*, M. Scott Peck, M.D. states,

> For many years it has seemed to me that human groups tend to behave in much the same ways as human individuals—except at a level that is more primitive and immature than one might expect. Why this is so—why the behavior of groups is strikingly immature—why they are, from a psychological standpoint, less than the sum of their parts—is a question beyond my capacity to answer. Of one thing I am certain, however: that there is more than one right answer. The phenomenon of group immaturity is—to use a psychiatric term—'overdetermined.' This is to say that it is the result of multiple causes. One of those causes is the problem of specialization.

In a truly mature and positive environment, group projects can be highly innovative and synergistic. If the environment is not one which is trusting and nurturing, group members may have trouble connecting their ideas due to poor communication skills, inflated egos, cult politics or tunnel vision of their own specialized area. True brainstorming is truly creative and when used in a non-judgmental atmosphere can give birth to great concepts and ideas. Even though this concept has been discussed in the literature and implemented by consultants for years, *Corporate Cult* dynamics will only sabotage a group's creative energy and focus.

Let's Do Lunch

Does your work group go out to lunch regularly? Are you invited? Do you go and if so, do you enjoy yourself? I have always been fascinated by the dynamics of lunch in *Corporate America*. For me and many others this is a lose-lose situation. I remember being approached for lunch many times. I have always been concerned with health and diet issues so I often brought my lunch or went to specific places which served the type of food which I wanted to consume. The luncheon invitations would go like this: "Do you want to go to lunch with us?" "No, thanks, I brought my lunch." This was very threatening to some peers because they were afraid that the boss would think that I was working harder than they were. If I decided to take a step toward "being more social," I would ask, "Where are you going?" The answer would frequently be the name of a restaurant that I didn't care to go to due to my strong feelings for health food versus fast food. I would briefly suggest another place with healthier choices, yet I would often be ridiculed or taken up on my offer and then ridiculed during lunch. Sometimes I just really wanted to see what went on at these lunches so I would agree to go to any restaurant only to find that nothing went on at lunch.

What I mean is, nobody talked. No wonder they wanted me to go. I have always been at ease, in fact overly at ease, with initiating or carrying the conversation. Nobody talked. They were afraid that self would come out or were they simply socially ill at ease in non-work related interactions?

Even work discussions were minimized because it was just too tempting to expose one's values and senses. I stopped going to these lunches realizing that I would pay a price for my non-attendance because they were just too boring. I had two choices:

I could either do the talking and have a good time which meant incriminating myself and "getting into trouble," or I could just eat and shut up, which I could do at the office in privacy. Sometimes I would decline invitations with the truthful excuse that I had lunch plans with a friend or friends and this was ill received. Friends who did not work for the company were considered non-cult members and should not be socialized with during the day.

I actually did have a very good friend who was hired the same day on which I started. She and I worked in the same department from time to time but there were even snide comments made about the two of us going to lunch together. It was more likely obvious to many that our friendship was real and did not include gossip, back stabbing or empty conversation. Because it was real and based on feelings of trust, it was threatening to the cult. As I tested the waters with honest disclosure, I realized it was a mistake. Their smiles and laughter generally accompanied my refusal, as they stated that "we just aren't good enough." It was not comfortable.

Parties

This one is my favorite. These parties were usually given and attended by people whom I would not want to sit next to on a bus, yet I went. I went because I was supposed to go and it was written in my job description in invisible ink. It was also in that rule book which nobody would show me. I eventually stopped going because I could not stop setting myself up. I felt that I performed at work and during work hours in a cult role. After hours, even great actors get out of role. Those who don't are more prone to nervous conditions. Being out of role was unacceptable and very dangerous. It provided a wealth of information for character assault. Some parties were for no reason, some were for promotions and retirements, and some even for the holidays. Imagine sharing Christmas cheer with the cult! What a paradox. When I was a single woman, I felt that I was wide open to feedback from the cult. I began listening to the feedback. The more I listened, the smaller and less vital my power became. My soul had begun its journey out of my body and I was soon to become a cult zombie.

I spoke to a man who worked for a corporation very much like my employer and he told me a story of a small-dinner party. He had been invited to a dinner party hosted by his CEO. He said that he left the party during dinner because he just couldn't take the "sick behaviors." At the party, he did not know many people but initiated a few conversations. One in particular was with a female employee who worked in a department in which he had once worked. They chatted, but as the CEO got closer to them in his rounds, the woman seemed "so mesmerized" and in awe that she began totally avoiding my friend and kept her eyes on the CEO as though he were an idol. When Mr. CEO finally did approach them, she talked with him about her family and children. My friend said he could tell that the CEO didn't hear a word of it. This was later verified for him when, during the dinner, the CEO asked the woman if she had any children.

Shortly after this, my friend left because he could no longer take the plastic environment of a pretend party, which really evolved around worship of the cult master. The party had originally been planned as an informal way to "get to know the staff." The dialogue occurring during the meal was a monologue given by the CEO who seemed to have no intention of involving his guests. Interestingly my friend told me that he blames the group, the staff, and not the CEO. His rationale was that we all like to talk about ourselves and feel that we are the most interesting topic. Because of this, he felt that if the "audience" had adjusted their attitudes, the CEO may have been forced to adjust his attitude and treat them more like real people who had separate lives and identities. The cult has this way of stripping us of self, if we let it. By not respecting ourselves, we greatly minimize the chance that anyone else will.

Cult Leagues

It would be wrong and inaccurate to say that softball and the like are clearly cultist, when in fact, these activities can be healthy stress-relieving events. They can allow employees to be together in a real activity. There is another side. Throughout my career, but especially early on, I was instructed, encouraged, and finally ordered to attend softball games as a player.

Although I exercise daily, softball has never been my forte. I began attending games, but because of such vivid and offensive comments made by males regarding the anatomy of female players as they ran, I stopped going. I began teaching a few evenings a week at local colleges and universities, and felt that this was a valid excuse to avoid games. It was then suggested that I attend the victory parties after the games.

These parties included lots of drinking and gossip. As far as I could see, this was a good way to get myself into trouble, so I gave those up too.

Corporate Dress

I think that books which rigidly discuss business dress have contributed to the narrow mindedness of the white collar *Corporate Cult*. The white represents sterility and white in the Nazi Aryan sense. I recall getting a dress code memo at a meeting. I could understand certain parameters dealing with a neat look, but it was clear to me, in my opinion, that personal boundaries were clearly overstepped. One sheet read, "only natural fabrics shall be worn, those of cotton, silk, linen, or wool." I would have been less offended by a company uniform. I enjoy wearing these fabrics, but the actual fabrics have nothing to do with the message requiring everybody to become a clone, "Stepford" manager, or a robot. What would come next? Would all of our children be ordered to attend a certain school and would we live in barracks? What if someone dared to wear a synthetic blouse or a color which had not been included in the corporate color code of blue, grey, certain browns and tans, and occasional blacks on certain clothing pieces. Appropriate haircuts and jewelry were also suggested.

The following year, we were told what type of cars we needed to drive. By and large these very strict standards have been relaxed. The change was initiated by Madison Avenue with the consensus of the American people. I realize that many organizations have gone to casual dress, and this too has issues. Some people feel more vulnerable. For some it works. This issue has to do with personal boundaries, and it is more important than most realize.

I don't know how many of these areas to which you can relate, but I do know that I experienced extreme cases. I want to affirm that I realize that each corporation is like a family unit. Each has strengths and weaknesses and some are healthier than others. Some group projects, teams, meetings and other dynamics may truly encourage employee well being, life and enlightenment. Others simply do not and these systems can affect people in a most damaging way if one does not exercise one's power and nurturing tools.

My very being was the antithesis of the corporate mold. I failed test, after test, after test. This made my experience magnified and obvious. I was lucky. For many, it is not obvious but much more insidious. Every time you give up your identity, the less you see. The veils and webs are so opaque and elusive, you'll have a hard time cutting through them. Sometimes the roles and behaviors that one needs to adopt in order to remain in the cult are actually very enticing and even sexy. They have an evil intrigue as did the decades old J.R. Ewing character.

In the *Corporate Cult*, some very *weak* ones stay. Some very *strong* ones stay. The *passive* players are not shallow enough to play by cult rules, though they are not strong enough to actively resist the *Corporate Cult*.

The *passive* players are the most affected and the saddest of all. The *weak* ones have consciously decided to stay and play because they cannot imagine original thought. They know that they cannot exist under any façade of power or societal validation without the cult. When they were children, they didn't say, "When I grow up I want to be a yes man." This has even been on television commercials, but as a kind of joke. The *strong* ones hold positions of power in the *Corporate Cult*. It validates them. It makes them *whole*.

Most of the people in the *Corporate Cult* are *passive* players. They have surrendered on a conscious level, though their subconscious begs for a time of originality and creativity. Because of this unresolved conflict (that our long commutes allow us more time to contemplate), we find stress, distress, disillusion, anger, rage and ultimately violence.

We hold on because we need money, and leaving to exercise our creativity or become more comfortable is often impossible based on our mortgages and other bills. Or, it is just a social mistake. Some believe that if you stay in place and wait long enough, your job or boss or situation at work will change and you will not have to exert the effort to initiate change? This can happen but why let the system victimize you until it changes? Only by taking responsibility for making the change happen within your person, will you be truly and eternally free of the golden handcuffs.

Survival and Transformation Strategies

1. **Employ humor into your life.** Throughout a stressful day, stop and ask yourself: "How serious is it? Who will die? Will someone I love be injured?" This will help you keep your job crises in perspective. Remember to have serenity. Accept what you cannot change, change what you can with courage, and be wise enough to know the difference. Ask your Higher Power for guidance with this.

2. **Try to be more flexible, open-minded and accepting with others.** Do this without sacrificing your self-esteem or

needs. I avidly feel that one should hold onto his/her center and identity, but one can do this without cutting off from reality.

By doing this, you will only help yourself. Think of someone with whom you work, whom you dislike or better yet, don't care for. Now imagine finding out that this person is a long lost sibling or parent. Would your acceptance or views change at all about this individual? There is no right answer. Simply note your response.

3. **Accept that performance does not always matter.** Impressions, agenda, and perceptions generally do matter. When you accept and digest this, it will be easier to survive in the system, for this is often one of the rules. When you understand this rule, you will lose your will and waste energy arguing over the strengths and weaknesses of your position. When this acceptance occurs, you will be able to raise the price of "your" stock through other means.

Personal Journaling

CHAPTER TWO
Slipping On The Corporate Ladder

No instinct tells him what he had to do, and no tradition tells him what
he ought to do; sometimes he does not even know what he wishes to do.
Instead he either wishes to do what other people do or he does what other
people wish him to do.

Viktor E. Frankl, *Man's Search For Meaning*

There are countless experiences in which I was challenged and threatened by the sterile left brain dynamics of *Corporate America*. I don't mean that my work was challenged or that they told me that they would kill me or fire me or steal my firstborn. I am talking about being personally challenged and threatened; my reality, my essence, my value system and my intuition. Some of these situations were so bizzare that I really wish I had video taped them.

The first notable incident occurred very early in my corporate career. I had been out of graduate school and working only about a year when I had my first heavy encounter with sexual harassment. Sexual harassment goes on rampantly and can mean anything from a peer commenting on your legs, to an overt, insolent threat made by a boss. Although sexual harassment is totally unacceptable, it is common and even sometimes done out of ignorance. Some sexual harassment can be a kind of rape, or at least attempted rape. Some who commit this crime are indeed too sick and so maladjusted that they really need serious help from the medical and psychological and spiritual community.

I had an unforgettable experience regarding sexual harassment. I was in a management development-training program and it was designed to last one year. At the end of one year, each trainee was presented, on paper, by his or her "mentor." A vote was cast that would rank the trainees. This was a final presentation. Everything depended on the ranking; your salary, potential raises and career paths. The presentations that the mentors performed were done approximately every month. Of course, each of the trainees wanted to know where "they stood" but were told nothing. They were rarely given even a little feedback, even when they asked. I don't know why.

My class started with about 15 trainees. This group narrowed down to ten by the time the year had expired. Some were fired; some reassessed their compatibility with the *Corporate Cult* and redefined their career as opposed to redefining themselves: a wise move. My boss or mentor, and I use the term mentor very loosely, was a very bright, hard-working and rigid man who had worked his way up through the ranks. He had not been to college and that seemed to be an issue for him. There were occasionally unnecessary comments made that related to my credentials and reminders that although I had more education than anyone in the district, I was still in need of a lot of growth, learning, and experience. He was right, except his tone was often defensive and my education was made a topic too many times.

I remember him commenting on a well known female actress and playboy model being the perfect woman and a great idol for women to model. I ignored this information and went on about my job. I remember being so very frustrated in my relationship with my boss because I wanted to have a truly mentoring relationship. Instead of nurturing and growth, I spent a great deal of time guessing. I allowed his mood swings to throw me off balance. I took much of it very personally and worked countless long hours into the evening to compensate for "whatever I did not know."

Later I realized that his actions toward me were meaningless, because in his eyes we had no relationship. I perceived that we did. It was true that he was my boss and I took directives from him, but he only related to me in terms of discharging orders. I naively bought into the mentoring concept.

Although he was my official boss and reviewer, I was also assigned a peer-boss who was at the level for which I was training. He assisted in my training and allegedly in my mentoring. He was very political and tried desperately to mold me into a cult employee. We had bold disagreements. I was too new with the company to realize that "I shouldn't speak my mind." He would often tell me that my boss, who was also his, wanted me to do thus and so. This was uncomfortable and seemed somewhat unfair, since he was my peer and heavily participated in appraising my performance. We were in competitive positions for raises and advancements. He also had quite a heavy influence over many female members in the group, a following so to speak—politically.

Three months before the final presentation and peer ranking was about to be made, there was a big party after work in honor of a new product. These parties were frequent events and I resisted them like the plague. However, I was consistently told that if I wanted to advance, hard work would not take the place of politicking at parties and playing on the coed softball league. For once, I decided not to be the odd man out and joined the activity. I went to the party. It was held at a local hotel and included dinner and cocktails. At the party I was introduced to a man who worked at my boss's level, who had been recently hired into the company from another firm. He had, so I was told, the reputation of being a genius and would soon become the CEO. I was rightfully impressed and decided to talk with this man. I had been told that he had been a priest for many years and was now married with several children. He had been assigned to an office on the other side of the state, and was only in town for the meeting.

We talked as people do at these meetings and he mentioned my progress in the training program and said that he heard quite a presentation about me, given by my boss. He said this in a rather uncertain tone, so I decided to clarify what exactly he meant. When I did so, he replied with, "There is something that you need to know if you are to stay in the program." Of course, my mouth dropped at his ominous tone. He told me to meet him in a particular room after the party and said that is would be "unsafe to discuss it here." He gave me a room number. I was so confused but thankful that someone would finally give me some solid feedback on my performance. The party dragged on and on and I decided to leave since I lived only two miles from the hotel.

I went back a few hours later, in my business suit, to meet this mysterious man at the designated room. I was naively shocked to find that "this room" was *his room*. To this point, whenever I had tried to use my instincts, feelings or ideas in the *Corporate Cult*, I received very negative reinforcement and was told that I must be paranoid, too emotional, a frenzied or hysterical woman, or illogical and totally irrational. I knocked on the door of his room and he answered the door and asked me to enter. When I did, he asked me if I wanted a drink and I declined. Then he sat on the bed, took off his jacket and tie, and unbuttoned his shirt. I began having some extremely serious doubts about his intentions, but being a real goal achiever, I persisted with questions regarding what he had told me. I was a walking metaphor of all the books on "How to Get Ahead in Business." I had read them and planned to carry out their orders. It was my belief that I was about to engage in appropriate corporate politicking.

He began talking in riddles. They made no sense to me at all. I became frightened and told him so, yet I can only realize now how ineffective that was. He tried to hypnotize me to talk and walk like a chicken. He then wanted me to repeat after him, "I will sleep with you, I will sleep with you, I will sleep with you." I had never experienced anything like this in my life. Had I stepped into another realm of reality, was he breaking down before my eyes, or was this just plain real?

He did not make physical advances toward me, so I guess that is why I stayed as long as I did. He explained to me that he came to town periodically and that I was to set up an affair schedule and that if I did this, he would ensure that I was ranked "1" in my class. If I did not, he told me "that he would ruin my career forever." I was stunned. This is the kind of stuff you hear about or see on television. It doesn't really happen to people, not Catholic girls like me who "work hard and had a good education and really never do anything wrong."

Once it really sank in and I realized what this guy was all about, I told him very cavalierly to, "Do what you will, I will never sleep with you and I will never have my career ruined. I am a great employee and I work very hard. I paid lots of dues to get where I am and I am not going to sleep with you tonight, tomorrow, or ever." I headed for the door and left. When I got home the phone was ringing and it was this man. He began his hypnotic chant about me sleeping with him and said "or you will be sorry." He then demanded that I meet him for breakfast.

I could barely sleep but I did not want to call anyone because I did not think that anyone would ever believe me. It sounded all too strange, especially the part about walking like a chicken. I could hardly believe it myself. I put on a stiff upper lip and went to work the next day, acting as though nothing had happened. In the office, many were speaking of this mystery man and how brilliant he was and how he was really on the track. I felt differently.

That morning, much to my surprise, mystery man came into the office to meet with my boss. I was terrified. After his meeting, he circled my crew and our work areas in a predatory manner. He then came into my office and closed the door. He began to make the repetitive statements, "You will sleep with me, you will sleep with me, you will sleep with me." Thank goodness, an account in my area needed immediate attention, and the supervisor of the account came to the door, knocked and stuck his head in. This gave me the excuse I needed to get rid of this maniac, at least for the time being.

The harassment continued for about six weeks. He would call me at home and sometimes at work. When he was in town, he would visit my office. I didn't feel that I could go to my boss. He was a conservative and rigid guy who blindly believed in the system. I knew that he worshipped this man. I knew that by telling my boss, I would really put the spotlight on myself. I couldn't go to HRM because at that time, there was no real system in place for employees who anonymously and confidentially needed to disclose. Going to HRM would have been like telling my boss. A few people who worked for me suspected that something was happening and they probably thought that I was indeed having an affair with this man.

I decided to take the bull by the horns and threaten him. The next time he came to town he demanded that I have lunch with him. He usually did so and I usually declined. This time I accepted and felt that I would put an end to this harassment in a public place where there would be witnesses and close-by onlookers. I refused to drive with him so we met there. We sat across from each other at the table and I looked him square in the eye and asked him to tell me exactly what he wanted me to do. After all that had happened, I still doubted his motives.

Part of me believed that he was giving me some secret stress test to see if I was really tough enough to climb the corporate ladder. I felt as though I was taking a final exam. God knows how I tried to not believe what he was saying, but when he precisely stated, "If you don't sleep with me, bitch, you'll lose your job and you'll never get another one. I can see to that. If you tell anyone, nobody will believe you. What choice do you have?"

He had a damned good argument. I looked straight at him and said, "I will never sleep with you. I will not lose my job and I feel very sorry for you and especially your wife. You can try to destroy my career, but I will tell your boss if you ever come near me again, or call me." He told me that I would never do such a thing and believe me, I did not plan on it. He began raising his voice and his face turned beet red, as I got up, walked out, never having eaten lunch.

I was worried because I knew that he believed me, though he knew that I hungered to do well at work. I was desperately seeking success. I am almost surprised that the thought of sleeping with him never once crossed my mind as even a remote possibility. I had no idea how and when, or if, he would sabotage me.

About a week later, I was riding my bike in the apartment complex in which I lived and I saw my boss's boss. He was relocating from another city. The company had put him up in an apartment while he awaited his family's arrival. Ironically, he had been hired into the company as a candidate for the same Fast Track Program on which I was hired; it had worked well for his career. I decided to take advantage of this fortuitous opportunity. It felt safe.

I told him all about the harassment. I got the sense that he was a more open-minded and a more realistic man. I felt relieved after I told him and I knew I had done the right thing. He turned to me and said, "But why didn't you go to your boss first?" What the heck was I going to say? "Well, because he is a narrow-minded, inflexible, rigid womanizer?" Instead I said, "Well, I didn't feel that it was appropriate for a subordinate to give one's boss this type of information about one of his own peers. I didn't see this as professional protocol." The man harassing me had been a peer of my boss and this answer seemed to make sense and carry some truth. I scored an A+ and he said he would take care of it and that I would never have to worry about the incident again.

Later I was ranked number one in my class, and two years later, the man who had harassed me still held the same job until he was fired because of sexual harassment. After the initial case was filed, over fifty women came forward to testify against him. The brave woman who finally turned him in was employed by a temporary agency and had little to gain by keeping his perverted secret!

I had thought of going forward but by then I figured the guy was in so deep, he was going to get what was coming to him. I was frankly still scared that somehow my name would be dragged through the mud for allegedly enticing him or being dumb enough to show up at his hotel room. I just didn't think that there was much to gain, so I let it go. This is a rare piece of corporate justice and it is quite apropos that a temporary employee brought on the justice and not a member of the *Corporate Cult*.

This poor man had lost his sense of balance somewhere between the priesthood and the *Corporate Cult*, or maybe even earlier. His act was so polished and on the mark, never missing a cue or line. It is hard to hate someone who deserves so much pity. What is truly amazing, is that I consider this man to be small potatoes next to some of the others with whom I've had to work.

Sexual harassment can be subtle or dramatic. Recently, a male friend of mine, who is a middle manager in *Corporate America*, approached me with a story, which he observed. He was disgusted. He witnessed a meeting in which a peer of his made sexually harassing comments to a female consultant who attended the session. Throughout the meeting breaks his peer, a married man, continued to say aloud in a teasing manner, "I wonder if Renee would go out with me." Initially, this could be perceived as teasing, but it is nonetheless inappropriate nonprofessional behavior. He continued to pursue her in this matter relentlessly. After the meeting a female peer informed her boss, who had been at the meeting but had not noticed the behavior, or the incident. The boss appropriately took it upon himself to approach and confront the harassing man, even though he was in another work group. The harassing man thanked the confronting woman, stating that he "had no idea that he had been menacing." Whether he was simply unconscious or feeding back the right lines does not matter. What matters is that he was dealt with appropriately.

My next career assignment entailed being transferred to a six-month rotational position on the sales assessment staff. This assignment was housed in HRM and was a temporary slot in which all managers in the marketing/sales organization served time. I had really looked forward to this assignment because I felt I had the ability to read people, generally liked them, and enjoyed relating to candidates. My M.A. in labor and industrial relations had allowed me to study many areas of HRM and hiring assessments. The position seemed very enticing and was indeed very interesting. The temporary staff serving with me was made up of a woman who had been on the staff for a year, a man from sales, and a man from marketing. We were all "supervised" by the director of the program who ran the assessment center. He was our same level so, in fact, was not really serving as our boss. Our official boss was his boss, even though we never saw him or had any contact with him.

This type of situation is very dangerous and is not atypical in the *Corporate Cult*. Multiple bosses and skip level accountability are excellent tools of manipulation exercised by the cult to relieve any one member of doing the dirty work or being responsible for one's mentoring. These types of organizations are dysfunctional. (It would be similar to having several mothers and fathers.) They generate and perpetuate confusion and illusion. I did not know that at the time, but later learned that these invisible bosses with lots of authority over one's career can easily destroy.

On the assessment staff, we would break into teams of two and go into small offices to conduct role-plays with potential employees. Each role-play was recorded and in addition to the tape, copious notes were taken about the behaviors of the candidate. I felt exhilarated to be working with human behavior for a change; with people who had not yet been polluted by cult behavior since candidates were just out of college. The assessment process, as it was ideally designed, was a good one.

At the close of each day, the staff would talk about each candidate with the use of notes and tapes. Each candidate would be ranked from one through five on various behaviors, that were deemed as critical to the sales job. It was the same process but a different assessment, the management assessment, which had lead to my hiring into the fast track program. Because of this, I felt especially committed to the process. As time went by and as I learned the process, I was very naive as to how it really worked, and tried to follow the format as it had been described. I took my notes, made my observations and played the roles. There were definitely times when my ratings disagreed with the majority, the others. Ties were not allowed and majority ruled although total agreement was the goal. I supported my points of view with conviction and learned to accept the fact that at times the group disagreed with me.

The director of the program was an elderly man who had a very serious heart problem and his heart was talked about a lot. People seemed to be really friendly and positive around him because of his illness, at least according to what the rumors said. I was comfortable with that until I realized that he was also granted "other privileges," such as showing extreme disrespect for women. There were countless questions made to me about my love life, my dating life, my measurements and sizes. This would also go on regarding women who were going through the selection process role-play. The disrespect was not isolated to women, frequently men who went through the process were also "secretly ridiculed" for stuttering, being short, being of a certain nationality or racial group. I experienced this attitude as being in extremely bad taste. No one else seemed at all offended by this type of immature and unprofessional behavior. In fact, they gleefully partook, except for the other woman who just smiled a lot. She was the only black member of our team and I wondered if she ever felt insulted. When I got her aside to probe as a possible ally, I was immediately given the cold cult shoulder.

One of the men on the staff decided to start confiding in me the details of his marital problems. Little did I know that someday soon, it was all going to lead to a plea to me to be his mistress. He actually followed me home on about five occasions and tried to force his way into my apartment. I creatively solved the problem by inviting people to my home immediately after work or I would leave the apartment, professing to have plans. Once I called the police just to scare him. He eventually backed off and became noticeably hostile to me at work. The atmosphere was most unpleasant and became much worse. The staff was small and getting along with the other members was necessary to stay on the job.

One evening I stayed late to do some extra work and I overheard the director talking about me to his boss. They were in his office and the door was slightly open. They must have thought that everyone was gone. The director began by telling his boss, who was my boss, about "my behavior." He began telling him that my write-ups and ratings did not agree with the way he saw things. I remember him saying, "She came so highly recommended with such high evaluations and education. We were told that she was the cream of the crop. If that is so, then why doesn't she see things the way we do." I was flabbergasted! I still believed that I was hired to think and not to fall into the norm like a robot. It was still my understanding that it was my responsibility to add a fresh perspective.

Perhaps my precognition was getting in the way. I saw too much, definitely more than they did. Today it is called emotional IQ or perceptiveness. From that moment on I decided to conform and began cutting out all small talk with the staff, not that there had been much up to that point. The next morning when Mr. Director told me that my legs looked sexy, I just gave him a cool professional grin.

When the assignment was over, I received an average rating. It stated that I had come into the assignment full of enthusiasm and that I became more detached and did not conform to the group's view of candidates in some cases. I asked my "boss" why this peer of mine was able to sabotage my appraisal without giving ongoing corrective feedback so that I could alter my alleged faulty behavior and performance.

My boss looked me dead in the eye and said, "You are absolutely right, and I am sorry." I said, "Oh, so you are going to change the rating." And he said, "No way." I responded, "But you said . . ."; he replied, "Yeah, I agree with you but I am not going to change the rating." This is unfair, it is hypocritical. "This is the HRM department, of all places. How can you conduct this type of organization?" I asked. He looked at me and responded, "Now I've listened to you and now I have a meeting, so I will have to ask you to leave my office, and I am sorry." It would have been too difficult to challenge his director. Since I was about to transfer out of the department and he would never have to deal with me again—the easy way out.

I was transferred back to the marketing department after my six months had passed and I was given another fast track assignment to manage a new product line. There were about twenty people chosen to take this track and only about half would make the final cut. There were numerous classes I needed to take. They were all very technical. I really didn't want the job, but I did like my new boss. He was sexist but not chauvinistic, if that makes any sense. I felt that I could work for him effectively because he seemed to deal upfront. He had little invested in sabotaging anyone's career.

When he asked me how I felt about the assignment, I admitted, "I had some reservations." He replied, "Oh, with all of your degrees and schooling you aren't one of those people who fall apart in technical studies?" I was in the process of taking course work toward a doctorate degree. Well, I wasn't about to say, "yes, and furthermore they bore me," because the thought of leveling in an honest way was too intimidating for me. The manipulative tactics worked. I "behaved" and did as I was told, for fear of the unknown consequences. This gave my boss an easy out. He never had to really be a mentor or manager, nor did he have to assist me in career development. He used manipulative cult dialogue, and I allowed it and reinforced it! So I said, "Oh, no, not me, I am just concerned about all of the travel entailed." The schedule was quite rigorous, gone for two weeks, every two weeks. The classes were given at offshoot locations all over the country at various prestigious campuses.

Swallowing all of my reservations and resistance, I plunged into the assignment and started programming my brain for systems operations success. I worked very hard during these classes. I found the material to be so dull and so incredibly boring, in fact the direct antithesis of anything that I ever wanted to do. Because of this harsh reality, it took me twice, three times or maybe longer, than anyone else to study, or so I believed. I remember celebrating my birthday one Super Bowl Sunday in an Atlanta hotel room with a computer. I was all alone in every sense of the word.

The next day the test came and I aced it. I received the second highest score in the class. Afterwards I went to the bar with a few fellow classmates to celebrate. In the bar I encountered a fellow manager from my home location. He must have heard the news of my high test grade. He looked at me and howled out in an extremely intoxicated manner, "Hey, who did you have to sleep with in order to get that grade, you cunt." What a collegial kind of guy.

Maybe that was one of my problems, I could never really take these vipers too seriously because they were truly laughable. The reality is that even though humor came to my personal rescue, these events had very little comedy. They were more tragic. I looked at him in amazement and left the bar. If only he had known that I had spent the night with the big white bear that I had received as a birthday gift. I later discovered that he was badly in need of recovery. This man was an alcoholic and had been suspended for drinking during working hours.

During this assignment I supervised a group of four men who ranged in age from about five years older than I, to near retirement. There were occasional disrespectful comments and obvious petty power struggles, but overall it was a pleasant and competent group of people. Two of the four asked me to have affairs with them. When I refused there was no harassment or repetitive nagging, only occasional innuendoes. Although technically this too was sexual harassment, I felt it was managed and did not threaten me. All of the four men were married.

When I was almost ready to complete the program, something changed. I had been doing quite well and was very proud of myself for sticking it out, although I still lacked the passion in my appreciation for the computer and programming field. The change was that my boss who so avidly supported me and truly tried to mentor me was transferred out of the state. I was disappointed to hear that he was going to be replaced by a man with whom I would have rather not dealt.

A few years earlier, an incident had occurred where there was to be a presentation on a new company policy, which was extremely controversial. This man came to my boss and asked me if I could participate on the committee for development and actually help arrange the dynamics of the presentation. My boss agreed to loan me a few hours a week. We worked on the presentation for about four sessions in which I simply gave input in writing, which had been requested. The night before the presentation was to be held, he called me at my desk after hours and told me that he had decided to take a vacation and that I would simply have to give the talk to all of upper management and my peer group. I did not want to go through with it, but I was told by my boss that I would do a great job. It was an opportunity for exposure! It was very curious to me that he decided to take a spontaneous vacation to an island. Most plan such events and the company normally made employees schedule extended vacations months in advance.

I did the talk and to be honest I have very little memory of it. I do know that I asked people to hold their questions until the end so that I would have a crack at control and that went over like a flying camel. Overall, I managed to get through this stressful surprise, but I knew I never wanted this man for a boss. Although it was difficult, I really tried to go into the relationship with an open mind and give it a fair chance.

No more than three weeks into the relationship, he called me into his office. He showed me a job opening for a strategic planner doing futures studies with another division of the company. He told me that he wanted me to apply for it because he did not see me in my current job. When I questioned him as to why he did not see me in this job, he replied, "It is just not what I see you doing." By the time I got around to telling him about my high marks and the progress, that I had made in classes, I realized that none of those facts mattered. What mattered was that he wanted me out of that job.

I applied for the transfer and immediately began meeting some of the most wonderful people in the company. I actually became thankful that I was transferring and really began enjoying my work. For the next few years I worked for a fabulously brilliant real person. She now owns a consulting firm of her own and was one of the front runners in the development of Issues Management and Futures Research. She eventually left the company to take a prestigious position, which worked a great deal with Congress. I am very proud to have worked with her and under her direction for she taught me a great deal.

When working for her, I was able to temporarily leave the cult behind. My peers took their cues from her and everyone was very conscientious and open. When she left, we reported to her boss for a few months, until the company underwent a massive reorganization. I was given the option of relocation or placement at another division in my hometown. My boss's healthy organization had allowed me to develop some balance in my life, due to more predictable work hours and less travel.

Having a stable work life had made my personal life more stable and I did not want to jeopardize it by moving out of the state. I decided to stay put geographically and went with another division as a HRM manager.

Survival and Transformation Strategies

1. **Don't allow yourself to be bullied at work, even by your boss.** This will only undermine your self-esteem and self-respect. This included inappropriate or invasive comments and questions, sometimes even those said in jest. Prepare yourself with a standard set of responses to comments and questions that people may ask you in the corporate environment. These responses should be given politely, yet they will almost abruptly shift focus off of you. There is no reason why you should have to discuss any personal information or, in some cases, even information about your job. Here are some rebuttals for awkward questions:

    What do you think?

    Why do you ask?

    I have been wondering myself.

    I've been asked that question before, I wonder why that is? As soon as I find out, I'll let you know.

    Repeat the question and say, "What do you mean?"

    Be sure to use a calm and deliberate voice. It should be firm but not defensive. This can also work when faced with an intrusive statement.

For statements that seem unfair or intrusive one might reply:

I feel a bit uncomfortable hearing that from you....

I'll have to give the comment some thought.

Why would you make such a comment to me?

I appreciate your feedback, and although I disagree, I understand your position.

You can probably think of other healthy responses too. These statements are real, yet not directly confrontational so they foster real and *truthful* replies. Remember to do this gently, firmly and in a friendly way. Know that if you tell people what they want to hear and not what you believe, there are consequences. The consequences may confront you unexpectedly and when you are without mental and emotional protection. Make your own choice, but be aware of the consequences you may pay later for sacrificing a piece of self.

2. **Ask for feedback on your performance.** Do this at least three times a year and do it in writing. Be sure to document your requests and responses. Do not accept vague meaningless statements that do not add up to concrete and simple declarative statements. This may alarm some supervisors or make them paranoid, so be sure to do this in a non-threatening way. One suggestion is to prepare a brief letter to your boss, under the guise of needing help with prioritization of ideas. State that you want to provide him or her with your best possible performance. Honestly tell your boss that your goal is to do well and make sure that the company gets the effort from you which they deserve.

In writing, this is an especially powerful tool and document. Even if you already enjoy your work situation, it will probably help your career.

3. **Don't allow anger or any negative emotion to immobilize you.** If you find that you cannot let go of anger or frustration that arise during or from the interaction, write down exactly why you are feeling anger, fear, hostility, and rage. This can be a brief note or a few pages. Fold up your note and toss it into a private box, vase or basket. Know that when you put it there you are letting go of your negative emotion and are open to a solution. Recite an affirmation as you do this. For example, "I, [your name), release myself from this situation and now shift my focus to grin and learn from it." This will produce amazing results by empowering your psyche and programming your mind to responsibly handle stressful situations in a calm and safe, feeling way. Upon occasion, you may have to wait until you get home from work to write the note, but do it just the same. Consistency helps! (Affirmations are discussed in greater detail at the close of Chapter 8.)

4. **Gain focus on yourself.** Become internally focused, not externally focused. Only you can adjust your perspective. Do this by listening to your senses, the very ones the cult is trying to capture. Do a body check. Use the chakra system as a monitoring plan. Visualize the rainbow colors in your body: a red rotating ball at the tip of your spine, orange just above it around your colon area, yellow at your navel, green in your heart, blue around your throat, purple between your eyes and white on the tip of your head. As

you visualize this, if any of the colors seem "off," or dull; or if they have any characteristics that seem odd to YOU, you can be pretty sure that stress has impacted you in this area. Remain internally focused and visualize the stress being eaten by your dog, your cat, or some other friendly critter, and free yourself of cult stress.

5. **Feed yourself positive talk.** Don't allow yourself to engage in negative thoughts. It is difficult at first, but you shall eventually shift. Use symbols if you want to reinforce your behavior. Placebos and rituals are very effective. For example, place a glass of water on your desk each day and tell yourself that any negative energy around you will go directly into the glass and thus be dissolved. At the end of each day, throw the water down the drain and clean the glass. Don't drink the water or use the glass for anything else.

6. **Have a plan.** Make yourself a work plan. Something brief and casual yet genuine. This is not to be cast in concrete, but it will serve as a check and balance system. It will get you thinking about your career aspirations, life priorities and career preferences. Reviewing it quarterly may be able to help you back on your path even though others may try to pull you off. Today, people have many careers and many retirements. Retirement has an entirely new meaning, so do the plan! If often means doing work you like. Yes, jobs may be plentiful today, but so is "right-sizing."

Personal Journaling

CHAPTER THREE
Denying The *Corporate Cult*

You have the right to judge your own behavior, thoughts, and emotions and to take the responsibility for their initiation and consequences upon yourself.

Manuel J. Smith, Ph.D.

I was quite pleased to be placed in a new HR division. It gave me a chance to participate in staffing the newly formed subsidiary. I felt it was quite exciting, like giving birth. The energies to which I was about to give birth at times seemed to be more like those of *Rosemary's baby*. What happened to me in the next few years made any other negative experiences in *Corporate America* seem minimized. I realized that wherever one is and whatever one does, there shall always be challenging experiences and people who may appear negative.

They are like the coyote. Some refer to the coyote as the trickster or heyoka. The coyote will be there to make sure you learn your lesson, so he can be a friend, but if you give him your power or empower him, he may attack you brutally.

What I had dreamed of with starry eyes in graduate school was gone. The learning experiences had been valuable in my reframe, and certainly the money was ample. I had been able to get through most of the hurdles unscathed and with a great deal more insight. This was a big turning point.

I will never forget the day that I met my new boss. I had also applied for his job, but was pleased to find out a black male got it. I have always lived in integrated circles, including my elementary and high school education in the city of Cleveland. I was glad to see a black man get into a position of such power and was confident that our relationship would be strong. I felt that someone who "probably" understood the massive discriminations of society and the *Corporate Cult* could foster openness and integrity into the corporate universe.

Our first meeting occurred at a restaurant. He called together all of my peers to meet with him and discuss our mission. This happened while we were still on our previous assignments; a few weeks prior to the actual start up. He personally called me on the phone and told me where and when. My first thoughts of him calling me were very positive ones. I thought, *great, a man who can make his own calls and does not helplessly delegate to a clerk or assistant.*

As we went through our brief conversation on the telephone, I experienced some very strange insights, and I immediately began to block them. They were just too scary and unexplainable. What I mean is that he was talking into the telephone as though I was an answering machine. It reminded me very much of what I had experienced with "mystery man" and his attempt to hypnotize me. His voice was sterile and direct. When I tried to induce pleasantries, I mean after all, the guy was going to be my boss and I wanted to get along with him, he completely ignored them. In fact, he interrupted me, cut me off, and then hung up. These were not good cues, but I was consciously trying to stay open-minded, so I blamed the connection and figured that perhaps he couldn't hear me.

Then I fantasized that his boss had probably been close by and was perhaps giving him some pressure to hurry. I then decided to try to convince myself that he was a boss, not a friend or relative and didn't have to be pleasant. But, he did owe me basic human respect. With some discomfort I attended the initial luncheon meeting.

I was the first person of my peer group to arrive. I introduced myself to this man, my new boss. My introduction and extended hand received only silence. His eyes were cold and narrow and bloodshot. I knew that he had been promoted into the position; I felt that it was only appropriate to congratulate him, and I did. This was not well received at all. He responded by telling me that he was the boss and that anyone who was going to work for him would be following his orders and then asked if I understood. I said, "Yes." He then told me that he had seen my "papers" and that "I seemed to have a lot of education," but asked if "I understood how to operate in a business." I was shocked, disappointed, and definitely not looking forward to my new assignment. My peers arrived and everyone seemed to function as though they had come out of the *Handmaid's Tale,* cookie-cutter people.

There were absolutely no pleasantries exchanged among peers, nor were there smiles. My new peer group consisted of veteran employees who had spent their lives with the company and paid many dues. Each one of them brought very specific areas of expertise and had a wealth of knowledge about their subject matter. I later heard that the "boss" had participated in hiring the other members of the group, whereas I was the odd man out, assigned to the group by "Corporate" and the executive board selection committee.

I have never been in the military so I can only imagine what it is like via movies, books, the media and personal testimonials from friends and relatives. The experience of working for this man relates very closely to all that I have heard. In fact, before entering graduate school, I became curious about the military and applied for a direct commission as a Second Lieutenant. After very rigorous testing and thorough examination procedures, I was granted a position in the officer-training program. After great deliberation, I decided not to accept the commission. Simultaneously, I had received an assistantship at Michigan State University and figured that the military would be there if I ever wanted to reopen the door. Well, here it was, and totally unexpected!

Individual meetings with this man involved him circling my chair in a predatory manner, as though he was about to pounce on me. This was an extremely intimidating tactic and was indeed intended to be. Whatever happened to the recent management theories stating that when bosses were talking with subordinates, or peers for that matter, they were supposed to step from behind their desks and sit next to them? This style immediately promotes true interaction versus a power struggle. By sitting next to whomever you are speaking, the subtext is automatically one of cooperation and openness. Team camaraderie more easily emerges.

Isn't it in fact archaic that in the 21st Century, we use labels like "my superior" and "my subordinate." Words are very powerful tools. Many business texts and gurus tell us that we are followers or leaders, yet we remain entrenched in boss and subordinate roles and references.

We should be using affirmations. They are commonly made up of words and visualizations, and are one of the most powerful components of our psyche. To address oneself as a subordinate and to address another as a superior surely has hints of a royal regime.

The *Corporate Cult* is our royal family. We do, in fact, need people at different positions handling different levels of responsibility. But why are they always labeled to sound so much like the caste system? The alleged or real levels of responsibility are what should be stressed about a position and not the title and "level." I guess it all relates to the worship of dollars. As we all know, it has been labeled "the root of all evil."

When I came into this man's office, who was called "my boss," I would often be told by him where to sit. He would then walk up to my chair until he was very close. He would then shove his face into mine and put his two hands on the sides of my chair, one on each side so that I couldn't budge. I have never been interrogated by the FBI, but it must be very similar. I have never seen agents Mulder or Scully use it! During one meeting he put his hand on my knee. It was actually my skirt since the skirt just covered my knee. He didn't leave it there very long. I was repulsed; and as he intended, effectively intimidated. Intimidated enough to ignore it.

These one-on-one sessions would last long after hours and there seemed to be little substance in them. In fact they really were not meetings. They could more accurately be called examinations or lectures. Since I had no performance problems, the "lectures" were usually about what I had better not do. This was the most perverse and ineffective type of corporate managing that I had ever encountered, on both his part and mine, I might add. I allowed it to occur.

My most vivid remembrance of this fine fellow is a closed-door meeting where he threatened to "transfer me to the most undesirable spot in the company," meaning both physically and career-wise, where I would be "far away from my family and friends." He promised that my career would be at a dead end if I caused any waves of any kind. Well, at that point, it didn't take a genius to figure out that my career was already at a dead end. He obviously did not want the product that I delivered to the company. Managers like this are so incredibly shortsighted. He was actually asking me to stop thinking and work as a robot, at his command. The company was paying me a high salary, or so I thought, to be creative and innovative and to take initiative. He then proceeded in a shouting voice with a list of specific situations, which would require me to break company policies and company rules. He informed me that I was never to ask questions and was to do exactly as he commanded.

A few evenings before this incident occurred, a coworker and I had been working quite late and were in the office alone with him. He was talking on the phone near our work area and this is what we overheard: "Don't worry, just put down anything, forget about qualifications and make something up. I am the boss and I will make sure you get the job." I suspected that he knew that I had heard these comments, even though I tried to become as invisible as possible and intently glared at my papers. What kind of man was this? Certainly nobody I would ever refer to as my superior. Unlike others who are just ignorant of basic management principles or very egotistical or domineering, this man truly seemed evil.

There were constant stories within the work group about his escapades and drinking sessions and ladies. He would occasionally ask someone to lie to his wife about a meeting should she call. We all have our frailties and the human condition itself represents non-perfection, but this guy did not have one redeeming quality that I could find. I had no respect for him on any level and I felt as though I was going to die.

This is indeed an extreme reaction, but not unusual for cornered and mistreated employees. It is the closest that I hope I shall ever come to being a hostage. This man began harassing me so much that others would mention it to me. I didn't know what to say. Although his rude behaviors were surely not exclusively for me, I clearly got more than a fair share. On some level maybe he knew that I could see who he really was and that I was not impressed, respectful or intimidated enough to kowtow; sadly a theme that began taking place in the work group. This is a very keen example of cult behavior. If you can't beat him, worship him, and I refused.

At Christmas I again naively decided that I might be able to begin a "new leaf" with this monster so I decided to buy him a gift. I wanted it to be something impersonal but something that could reflect a truce. I ended up making a modest donation to a charity on his behalf. When he found out that I had done this he came to my desk and said, "You donated money in my name. You probably did this so that you can get extra tax credit. Give me a slip marked tax deductible with my name on it." My mouth dropped open for minutes in complete wonderment. I said nothing. Who says reality isn't stranger than fiction?

During this period, the asthma I had developed got much worse. It became so bad that I would frequently see the allergy doctor twice a week. My "boss" would occasionally challenge this and set up meetings, which seemed to intentionally interfere. I worked countless unpaid overtime and rarely went out for lunch, so I felt his attitude was uncalled for, at best.

My ulcerous condition grew worse as well, so I began a conscientious health regime to restore my well being. During morning meetings, we were to take turns bringing donuts. When my turn came, although I brought donuts, I also brought several pieces of fruit. He ridiculed my fruit eating. Due to this, or so I imagined, no one else would touch the fruit. In retrospect, it all sounds like Adam and Eve, though he was the serpent.

During this assignment in HRM, I had many contacts with other satellite locations. They were staffing their respective locations. Not a day went by that I didn't hear from these liaisons how glad they were to deal with me and not my "boss." I would hear horror story after horror story and the punch line would always be, "How does he get away with it and why is he still on the job?"

In a few instances, the liaisons with whom I dealt were transferred to my group. Instead of gaining support, as I had hoped and expected, they following the rest of the *Corporate Cult*, dismissing what they had confided in me. They began to begrudgingly worship him and his blatant arrogance. They minimized their own realities. It was like a science fiction horror film.

During this time, except for the coworker with whom I had witnessed the unprofessional phone conversation, I had very little validation for my reality. I knew I was not imagining all of this, but how could everyone else deny it? The truth is, I now realize that it is much easier to deny a situation than to grasp the scary and unpleasant reality. I was in fact very lucky to be able to catch a glimpse of the truth. I was surrounded by people who were ready to turn on the gas, regardless of who was in the chamber, or their innocence.

The staffing functions were slowing down after a few months passed, and the company was in need of someone to organize and oversee the training and development function. My "boss" called me into his office one day and told me that training and development was my new assignment only because there was no one else in the district who had any experience in this area. I had taught seminars and classes at community colleges and was at the time working on my doctorate. This decision seemed to make sense to me, so without hesitation I agreed. I had truly liked the staffing function, and was very familiar with policies and techniques with my experience and a M.A. in labor and industrial relations.

I attempted to embrace the new opportunity. I hoped that the training and development job would give me a chance to have a more direct focus and a specific program to meet the needs of the company and the employees. Staffing seemed to only allow staffing managers to operate in a responsive mode, whereas training would allow me to respond to the company's needs while creating innovative programs. I felt that I would possibly be more isolated from my boss's constant stream of attacks. He took my staff away from me and assigned them all to the only other staffing manager.

The job was a new beginning for me and I tried to use the opportunity to immerse myself into the job while focusing on results. Upon countless occasions, I attempted to obtain agreement on a training plan or plan parameters with my boss. It was an impossible task. He always spoke in circles and I had little awareness whether he did this to sabotage my efforts or because he simply had no idea what he wanted.

I began a series of needs assessment interviews with various department managers, officers, and employees. This may not be true in other organizations. I quickly realized that the only group that cared about training and development were the lower ranks of employees. Much to my chagrin I became aware of the fact that at this company training and development was a "Barbie doll" assignment. It was something that nobody "who counted" cared about and something that was designed to have little impact. I also engaged in interviews with consultants in the field to see if there were any answers that could all make it go away. Each one who met my boss, even though unsolicited, informed me that he was the problem.

Over the weeks that followed, my "boss" started ignoring me. I don't mean occasionally or just not listening, I mean in an extreme way, such that I became embarrassed for him. In meetings, elevators, passing in the hall or group "social activities" he simply did not speak to me at all. This went on for a few months. I remember approaching him and he would either walk away as though I were invisible or he would give me his straight and narrow glare for a few seconds and then walk away. If someone had told me of this type of a story, I would have unquestionably believed that they were either exaggerating or had a very thin grasp of reality. This scared me. I was being given the cold shoulder.

On one occasion a peer of mine was confronted by my boss who wanted free tickets to a sporting event. My peer was involved in advertising and he frequently had tickets to major sporting events that were to be given away to customers. My peer informed my boss that he could not provide him with free tickets since the company policy had been to avoid free tickets, except when a customer was involved. At this point my boss began generously using the "F" word and began threatening my peer, saying that he would get even. On another occasion, he was caught by a secretary rummaging through her desk looking for free tickets. These incidents were called to the attention of another director, but there seemed to be little impact.

I played out many scenarios in my head regarding approaching my boss' boss. Since I was in human resources, I surely couldn't go to HRM to make the complaint. Perhaps I should have. If there had been a slim chance of empathy, I would have. These people bought into the *Corporate Cult* behavior and also did not want waves. Furthermore, they tended to be much older and clearly in the "good old boys" network. My boss' boss in particular was known for calling female employees "honey, sweetie, and dear." He also was a golf fanatic and would sometimes pick up his club and practice his swing while you were talking. I felt trapped. I couldn't see any way out.

I honestly didn't consider legal advice at that time and I am not sure why. I did not really believe that I could have solved the problem that way. And I guess I wanted to pretend that there was an amicable solution. I did seek legal counsel as a last resort. I considered looking for a new job, though my hours were long and I came home so drained, there was little time and inspiration to become involved in a heavy job search.

I had been in touch with one coworker who was positioned in a remote location. He gave me word that his department, corporate planning and development, was going to move to my location and because of my background in futures research, he suggested that I apply for a position in his group. It all made sense. I indeed contacted his vice president and set up a meeting with him and one of his directors. When I met with the vice president, I must say that I was not quite sure, at first, what to think of him—the "cult VP" who was not at all well-liked by the company at large but worshipped by his group. He was overly polite in a rather insincere way and pretended that he saw himself as a very innovative intellectual who was unquestionably for the good of the group. Sometimes he could also play the role of absent-minded professor.

A few days later I was able to make a training and development presentation for the corporate planning group and was able to observe the dynamics. After making observations, I decided to stay where I was. Yes, as unbelievable as this is, it is true. The difference was this. Where I was, although my boss was impossible, he did seem to highly regard my credentials. In some bizarre way I believe he respected me for this—deep, deep, deep down. Fantasy or reality, I believed this. Although he had worshipers in the group, they were more or less silent worshippers. The corporate planning situation was worship in a habitual sense. Everyone seemed brainwashed by the "cult VP." They literally and obsessively discussed the vice president, what he had on, what he ate for lunch, what he said about whatever. In their own argot, he was ceremonially proclaimed to be divine. Is the whole world like this, I wondered? By the way, for what it is worth, he was not charismatic.

By now I didn't feel whole. I felt like a hole. I watched the older employees, many proudly attesting to working through the night, showing up at the office the next day in the same clothes. Many compulsions existed within the group, as a group and individually. The atmosphere was very intense and I felt like a misfit. I received strange and curious glances, especially from the other female employees. It seemed as though they were jealous at the thought of having another woman join the harem. When I first had these feelings I initially discounted them. It was hard for me to accept, so I dismissed myself as paranoid. Yet, my instincts gave me a profound sense of knowing that I was correct.

I scheduled a meeting with my boss, HR man, and this time he did in fact talk to me. I told him that although I had an interest in the corporate planning group, I had decided to stay in this group. He quickly jumped in and told me that I belonged in the planning group because I was "so smart and educated." I told him that I did not want to go and he said, "Well, that's too bad because you start in three weeks."

I did not think that he was serious. I began to question why. Even though I did not enjoy working for this man, I had invested a great deal of time and energy in the job.

I see today that this line of thinking was only dysfunctional on my part. The entire system was sick. At some level, I denied this truth. If I had accepted it, I would more than likely not have chosen to relate to the system as if it were fair and healthy. It was a *Corporate Cult*; a faddish devotion exists when a *Corporate Culture* turns unhealthy, dysfunctional, unfair, unpredictable, beyond reason and abusive. The thought of me "proving my loyalty" was hardly less delusional than the battered wife or child who feels the beatings will stop if they can only be better or perfect people.

My boss went on to explain with ease that he never planned to give me a ranking above average and that I would be lucky to get that. He said that because he had at least three "old timers" in the crew with me, and because all rankings were forced into a bell-shaped curve, I would never be able to get to the top end stacked up against the "old timers;" politically it would simply never occur. His words were discouraging and enough to rip apart any American dreamer.

What made it even more ironic was that the "old timer" of them all was a woman who retired early, shortly after this conversation took place. As she was cleaning out her desk she disclosed to me how she had come to loath this man and detested him so intensely that she had decided to retire early. She had given her entire life to the company and couldn't bare to be treated with such great disrespect by an "incompetent district manager." I asked her if she had considered discussing the issue with someone at the vice president level. She assured me that she had considered it and was playing with the idea of writing to his boss, for whom she had worked, years prior. I strongly encouraged her to do so. Months later I discovered that she had not and I can't really blame her. After leaving the company, I was told that she was having such a good time, she could not spend even one minute or day stressing herself about negative activities from her past. I will never know what impact she could have made.

After hearing that my career would be on hold at an average rating, I immediately began making survival plans for my new job and desperately tried to look on the bright side.

"Impermanence surrounds us."

Zen Buddhism

Survival and Transformation Strategies

1. **Realize that your reality is just that—your reality.** Hold on to it because nobody else will protect it. It is your responsibility. Your reality doesn't belong to anyone else so don't expect anyone else to experience it. If you do not hold on to your reality, your judgment will rot! You can get a stronger hold

on your reality by sharing it with someone who can be trusted, preferably outside of the office. If you do have a safe relationship at work, then share with that person, but don't be careless in your disclosures. Act as if you were playing chess and attempting to protect your King and Queen. Calling up this image helps because you must, in fact, protect both sides of your reality. The masculine is represented by the King, which would include left-brain technical skills and logic. The feminine energies, represented by the Queen, are expressions, feelings, all sensitivity, and intuition.

It is often easier to forget key incidents and the fine details upon which a career is built. Invest in an inexpensive notebook or journal. Use it to record your truths and realities! Read them through once a week or once a month as a check or reference point.

2. **Don't believe that merely because something isn't just, it won't happen.** Accept and open your eyes to the injustice that occurs daily all around you. Stop denying it. By denying it, you only feed the cycle. Only by seeing it and accepting it can you begin to change or deal with it.

3. **Ask yourself what your job does for you and write down the answer on a sheet of paper.** Don't think of your time at work as doing your time. That is a life sentence approach. Unless you are incarcerated, you have at least some choice about what you do with your time and your life. On another sheet of paper, write down what you would like from your job. And finally, on a third sheet, record what you give to your employer that is of value. If you are honest and there is a

good balance between all three, then you are probably in a good career place. If your sheets are out of balance, you will want to look at what kinds of things you can do to create a more level scenario. This is also an upbeat way to assess your career since it focuses on the positives and not the negatives. But don't ignore those either. List them as well.

4. **Don't take "it" personally, whatever "it" may be.** Look beyond what seems to be the force. This is very easy to say but very hard to accomplish. No matter what kind of injustice is being directed at you, it is true that some of it *may be* personal, but much of it is probably because of the position you are playing or represent. We all naturally see the world through our own eyes, our own perspective. A comical story that might affirm my point goes as follows:

One day I drove by a world headquarters, located close to my home. I noticed that over twenty picketers carried large colorful signs outside the building. I stopped my car at the red traffic light and glanced over at a sign, and I read, "Pork is scum." I chuckled because I am now a strict vegetarian and I wondered why vegetarians and Orthodox Jews were picketing this corporation. I was just getting ready to give the pickets a wave of approval when I caught the sign again and realized that it said, "Porn is scum." I laughed for some time. I guess I spend more time thinking about meat than pornography. Take a second look and see what other people are *really* saying. Look beyond what seems to be the source. Corporate Culture fosters and nurtures the dysfunctions learned in unhealthy family settings. We all have our idiosyncrasies.

5. **Don't rely on employment law to protect you.** You may not
    be a protected class, and even if you are, many states have
    "at will" employment. Most importantly, the law is very
    separate from immoral and unethical behavior.

Personal Journaling

CHAPTER FOUR
All About Chess

If one believes it is possible to be logical, rational and objective, then one ignores the ways one is not and uses only a small part of the brain and senses.

Anne Wilson Schaef

Although not to my conscious knowledge, I had allowed the *Corporate Cult* to get into my driver's seat. I was a pawn. I could move my hands and feet and turn my head and talk and walk, but only where and how they wanted me to. I had surrendered by not trusting my intuition or my gut. I had bought into their system via subliminal persuasion. The pressing conformity was just too tough for me to tackle.

As I said earlier, I believe that these skills reside not in the rational mind but in the solar plexus; a "gut feeling" tells us when we are being lied to. But how can we receive messages from our built-in lie detection center when we numb it with alcohol, drugs, food, gambling, money making, and workaholism?

I was numb enough to be controlled by the system. I ignored my gut and began shifting my negative thoughts of fear over to positive thoughts, dreaming of successes and challenges which would allow me to contribute and help my career.

This technique of visualization and positive imagery has always been very effective for me and it is, in fact, effective for anyone when employed with persistence and determination. Consistency also helps. (I discuss the specifics of it later in the book.) Even in graduate school when I felt overwhelmed and I really needed to get out into the world and make some money, I made myself what I then called a motivation bulletin board. Most of my classmates who saw it in my room or on my desk thought it was curious and strange, or so they told me. On it I pasted pictures I had cut from magazine pages of beautiful clothes, a sports car, fancy jewelry, theatre tickets, and all types of material things I wanted. Low and behold the bulletin board was a great driving force for me, a real energizer. In fact, I managed to get all of the items on my bulletin board.

At the time I never realized how important, how vital, a bulletin board would be which had photos of the Statue of Liberty, pictures which reflected serenity, peace, justice, and ethics. Those intangibles that I couldn't cut out of a magazine and paste onto a board were the things for which I now longed. Getting them seemed so much more difficult and mysterious. The prices were deep, deep in my identity and ego. My later visualizations dealt with having a peaceful and fulfilling career. I wish I had done it much sooner.

When I was transferred to corporate planning, I was allegedly hired to do environmental analysis and futures research. I enjoyed this type of work and thought that the assignment would be peaceful and fulfilling.

The assignment entailed participation in a number of organizational meetings. The meetings were supposed to center around improving the organization. My initial understanding was that I would be spending about 25 percent of my time in meetings. As it turns out, I spent over 50 percent of my time in meetings and I served as a scribe—more like a secretary and gopher of the team. I had never been involved in a department like this. At first the concept sounded wonderful but we got so bogged down in the process. Instead of making the organization more effective, at the end of each meeting, we found ourselves at the same place we were before the meetings ever started. It is a very draining process.

In this new department, I was regularly harassed sexually, especially by two of my "peers." They were both married. One presented his harassment as a game, and the other tried to force himself on me. The latter one followed me home to my apartment. I had just gone inside and closed the door. Then there was a knock and there he was. I told him that I was very tired and didn't want any company and he forced his way in. I think he had been drinking. I later found out that he had an alcohol problem and drank during the day. (Yes, I know this sounds familiar from an incident in Chapter Two and the assessment staff.) I had only recognized that he was a chain smoker and perpetual coffee drinker. I would guess that he had many addictions. He said that he just wanted to talk because he felt that his career was being sabotaged.

In retrospect he was probably a *Corporate Cult* member who wanted to defect, but his alcohol gave him the "courage" and ignorance that he needed in order to stay. The real courage that he needed to leave would have only been his, had he stopped drinking and gained true consciousness. Maybe then he would have just been aware and helpless.

I reminded him that he was married. As I did this, I feared that I was making an "innocent thing out of nothing" because my feelings or realities had always been minimized in the *Corporate Cult*. I could hear myself now. "Can't you handle yourself?" The penalty for being naive was outrageous. I attempted to reason with this man who ended up "hitting on me" until I finally got rid of him by threatening to call the police. I still remember feeling so sorry for him the next day at work. I imagined how embarrassed and humiliated he must have felt, until he started the same thing over and over.

Once he finally realized that there was no chance that I would ever become involved with him, he changed his tactics and became very mean spirited, making regular personal comments to me. He would come up to my desk in the morning with some of his favorite opening statements: "So, who did you have sex with last night?" "Did you stay out all night?" "It looks like you didn't have time to shave your legs." "It looks like you're going bald." "There is a big part in your hair." "Your skirt looks a little tight, you must be gaining weight." "The job must be getting to you, I see your face is breaking out." He always spoke with a mumble, which seemed to make his comment even more loathsome. Finally, after believing that he wasn't going to go away, I decided to consult a few peers about his behavior.

They minimized it just as I had guessed and basically told me to keep a stiff upper lip. They tried to convince me that the comments were said in jest, only to get a laugh or smile out of me. And, since I didn't laugh, I must not have a sense of humor!

I began treating him as though he was invisible which eventually worked. After all, I had been treated as such by my former boss and understood the powerful impact. There were times when I had to go into meetings with this man and do projects with him. These experiences were unpleasant in every way. Later I got a female boss in the department and told her about his comments. She told me that it would be unprofessional for her to get involved and that it would show that I couldn't manage myself, so she just noted it and suggested that I give him the cold shoulder as well.

I was often put on study teams with many "good old boys." I was always "sweetie, honey, cutie, with great legs." The only thing that could have possibly made it worse was if I had been blonde, for I'm sure they would have added "blondie." I tried to manage these men in many different ways.

Sometimes I would be curt and that awarded me the title "bitch." Sometimes I would go along with it and try to believe that it was just their way and that underneath they realized that I had a brain and could actually think, being a MENSA member. This choice of behavior simply reinforced the "honey, cutie, sweetie" labels. Sometimes when I would ignore them, their response was "she is on the rag." This vulgar expression was sadly not uncommon for them to use.

There was no way out but out the door, but at the time I hadn't considered that possibility. It always amazed me that the married men were the ones who were bothersome and the single men kept to themselves. At least in my situations, the single men chose not to engage in demeaning talk about women, at least not to my knowledge.

I should have never allowed this belittlement to occur. This in no way excuses their rude behavior, but as a truly innocent young female manager, I had never anticipated such lessons nor had I been prepared for them.

My first boss in corporate planning was a man who disliked directness. He did not, however, allow his discomfort with it to keep him from putting people in their place. Ironically, he was a director.

I never, in a year's time, received feedback on my performance from this man. I tried to "pin him down" several times and it did me no good. He would make comments such as: "How did you feel about it; it was interesting, wasn't it?" "Why do you ask?" But I always knew that he was doing this intentionally. I also always knew that he knew that I knew that he was doing this intentionally. He was a true *Corporate Cult* master. He was so smooth and so slippery, I had even been forewarned about him by both men and women in the group. Others made comments about dealing with him. On the outside he reflected an excellent act of being a modern liberated executive who believed in equality among all. Behind closed doors he got his point across so subtly that one did not even realize what hit, until hours later.

Although I don't respect this type of managerial approach, I did admire him some for his ability to function in such a tricky manner. Eventually he slipped up and got caught and was fired. He was fired because he began having an affair with another departmental employee. Both were married and the relationship ended up being less than discrete.

Simultaneously to this, he began changing his role and image and actually began deviating from the *Corporate Cult* goals. Because of these dynamics, it is hard to tell why he really left. This man was brilliant and had the highest of aspirations. When he saw somebody getting in his way he tried to mold them to his way. If they declined, he got rid of them immediately and usually sent them directly into an enemy camp.

While working for this man, I never received a goal or directive. I decided to develop my own work plan and he approved. Night after night, I was invited out for a drink. I never once accepted. There was never pressure, at least never overt pressure. Invitations to "go out" were consistent and persistent, regardless of my refusals. I can only wonder if this didn't directly impact the fact that when appraisal time came, I was told my goals were not a meaningful contribution to the group and that my projects did not seem to be what he had in mind. I chose to not make waves by not pressing him for written agreement on my job plan. This is very similar to the choice I made to repetitively decline drink invitations without confronting why they kept coming. The fact is that when one is in such a situation or dealing with someone like this, one can only avoid the ultimate confrontation so long.

Never underestimate the fact that if you are playing someone else's game and if it is their rules that evaluate you, they can be changed to suit the situation. So, what is fair and right doesn't matter, nor does your performance matter.

This man saw to it that I was transferred to the other group in the department. It was headed by the director of development, a woman. These two directors were great rivals. This was not a secret, but often a display of aggressive disagreements and harsh words exhibited at staff meetings. During this entire period, although those of us working in the planning and development group were "working for" one of the two directors, we were allegedly all reporting to the vice president of the department who wanted us to believe that he saw the department without levels. This was merely a game. Although we were constantly told that the organization was without levels, there were many signs of levels in all forms: anything and everything from offices versus cubicles to executive parking spaces versus open parking, and, of course, salary, titles, and not being "allowed" to talk to management who were two levels or more above us! Simultaneously a "big study" was underway to redo all job classifications. As a result, jobs beginning at "top management" or director level received an increase in pay with additional bonus options; levels "below" the director title were, in many cases, downgraded and given increased levels of responsibility.

For a matter of months, there was a feeble attempt to give all of us the same title or make all of us sit in cubicles, including some higher salary ranges. This just ended up frustrating some who felt they had worked hard to gain a pay grade and wanted their perks. We all understood this and most simply wanted real respect, regardless of what "level" they were. We all began to dislike the hypocrisy and placating methods employed to superficially boost our egos.

Working for this particular female director did not come as good news to me at first. I immediately recalled a situation where we had both been assigned to a new product task force months before. One Saturday she stormed into my office and in front of another employee, who was my peer. She began screaming and aggressively throwing her hands about. She was upset that a certain piece of information had not been made available to her regarding the project. My initial inclination was to immediately defend myself, especially since she had overlooked the information and was, in fact, wrong.

I did not, however, defend myself because I had done so in the past and realized it just made one look and feel weaker. With that in mind, I simply and softly said, "I apologize for all of my faults and errors." Just as I had hoped, my calm and serene state threw her into a blazing tizzy. She seemed so appalled that I refused to meet her head on with a strong voice and a dramatic flair. She turned, red-faced, and stormed out of my office.

When she left, three other "team members" entered and questioned what happened. I said very little and went on with my work. About thirty minutes later, she reentered my office and began to apologize. She apologized about six times that day, literally. I felt sorry for her. I believe that her apologies were genuine. She had been upset and driven to wit's end by the *Corporate Cult*. Her stakes were higher than mine could ever be. I felt bad that she apologized, but the fact that she really overdid it, made me realize that my cool bothered her. She sensed a power about me that she wanted to shake. She implied this by referring to how well I handled myself.

I had been wary of this woman since that time and many in my group openly discussed how she disliked me. This was only based on the screaming incident, which they overheard. When I found myself assigned to her group, everyone seemed so interested in how

I felt and how we would fare. I decided, truly decided, that I was going to maintain an open mind and try to ally with this new female boss. I idealistically envisioned a woman camaraderie developing and perhaps even a mentoring relationship. During our first private meeting, I disclosed this and she seemed to sincerely welcome my attitude.

In her I saw much of myself. She was a hard worker, she did have a sense of reality about what went on, she was emotional, sometimes abrupt, crude and painfully honest. She was "sucked into" the *Corporate Cult* to the extent that she believed that she could transform it and that perhaps sometimes its methods would be for the "good of all." She was an attractive woman. I could see her pain through her talk of chain smoking, caffeine/chocolate addiction, and extreme in weight fluctuations. She tried so hard and was constantly overextended. The *Corporate Cult* took advantage of her often fresh perspectives and new attitudes. They set her up. Many times she was on display to do the dirty work and be the comic scapegoat. It was a very complex situation. I tried desperately to simply relate to her as my "superior," but the dynamics were just too intense and she knew who I really was. I knew who she really was. It was tough to pretend that we were just two other *Corporate Cult* members or refugees. I am sure that she saw herself in me.

Since we first met, this woman had encouraged me to leave the corporate world and enter a more creative field. I had mixed feelings about those comments. In some ways, I knew that she envied me because I was not in as deep as she. In other ways, I believe that she truly respected me and liked me, and wanted me to escape the claws of true corporate ladder climbing. She and other women in the department who probably had more "credibility in the cult" than I did, would frequently comment on my attractive appearance and tell me that I should be in another industry. One can only assess those types of comments with great care.

As time went by I actually became quite supportive of my boss and would, in fact, defend her among my peers from time to time. When this occurred, I was frequently ridiculed and challenged. I wonder if there would have been the same level of inquisitiveness had this boss of mine been a man. She was well set up and finally I realized that they sent her to set me up.

At one point I was put "in co-charge" whatever that means, of a team. This was usually the case in the department. Nobody was ever really in charge because the offenses could not be manipulated to protect favorites and incriminate the gutsy and innocent. I handled my duties as project co-chair as I saw fit and then one day about two weeks into the project, my vice president came to me gruffly and said, "I don't mean to sound ominous, but I just heard some very troubling things from one of your peers about your performance and it makes me very angry."

I was almost speechless and asked for clarification. He then told me that he had no time to discuss this with me and that he was on his way out of town to a meeting and would then be on vacation. He projected that he would not return to the office for three to four weeks. He then left abruptly and there I stood, amazed and confused. What type of professional behavior and demeanor was this and what good was it supposed to serve? With not even a clue in mind, I went to my boss. I could not imagine continuing on with the project without any support and now with a reason to believe that there was something wrong.

I first confided in another female peer who was in the department and much like my boss. What I mean is that she was part of the *Corporate Cult,* yet she could see what it did and in many ways despised it. In fact, she loved hating it. She would bad mouth it one day and cling to it the next. She had become a friend of sorts and I knew that at the very least, she would be able to empathize with my frustration. I think that she, too, was intimidated by me. Surely not because I would leap over her on the corporate ladder, but because like her, and like my boss, I saw the *Corporate Cult* for what it was. The difference with me was that I refused to join and constantly questioned norms and reality. It is no different than "liberty and justice for all." When any one of us are threatened in these areas, we are all at risk.

I was threatened and they were at risk and knew it. I was a constant reminder of the real world, or truth, of how the system masterfully manipulated one's strengths and weaknesses. She strongly encouraged me to talk to my boss. She and my boss seemed to be friends; at least everyone thought that they were, even though they did not socialize outside the office. A very odd thing occurred. I sat in a meeting with my boss and this peer from 5:30 that evening until almost midnight. It began as a usual session in which I desired to ask my boss about what her boss, the VP, had said to me. I wanted clarification.

My peer was present and before I knew it, the door was closed and a heavy-duty discussion began. I felt uncomfortable asking my peer to leave at that point. My boss seemed very comfortable with her there and at that point, I realized that it didn't really matter who was there, I just wanted to get some information. This six-hour session was quite demeaning and an overall waste. There was very little substance to most of the one-way conversation that took place; my boss talking at me. Although I came home that night and engaged myself in extensive documentation, I, myself, am still amazed that this type of event took place in a profitable corporation that allegedly employed management professionals. I, too, was at fault for even allowing this to happen.

The session began by me describing what the vice president had said to me. My boss next initiated a conversation about the vice president and his feelings toward me. She believed that he "did not like me." She felt that he had therefore begun an attempt to "get rid of me." The majority of the hours in this meeting were a rigorous monologue that explained why I did not fit the role of my job in any way. She stressed many times that I did not look the role due to my "petite stature and attractiveness." She told me that my training and education were meaningful, but not in her department and that I was in the wrong organization. This was perplexing for me because much of what she said was true, yet the setting and delivery seemed very unsuited for the situation.

She informed me that the company was restructuring the department and that eventually it would only consist of Harvard MBAs. She warned me that if I stayed, I would eventually be ranked so low that I would be forced out. She made the analogy that I was like a flower living on a desert and would eventually be "crushed by snakes." It was so difficult to discern whether she was indeed trying to finally give me another piece of reality or was she, in fact, like the coyote, being a trickster and playing a mind game based only on her fantasy. It almost seemed as though she expected me to break down and wanted me to cry.

Several times she stated, "I can't believe your composure, you can break down if you want to." I was actually too numb to feel much of anything and my primary goal was to get as much information as possible, and then analyze it later in a safe place. She shoved the tissue box my way several times, although I didn't need it. What an alien power struggle and for what were we really struggling?

Many times, I asked her if she in fact had heard her boss (the vice president) say that he disliked me. She denied it and would comment that he was too shy to discuss his feelings and didn't like to admit it when he disliked someone. She also swore me to secrecy and made me commit that I would not share any of the dialogue with him. It seemed odd that a man too shy to express feelings or opinions would become a vice president, but in the *Corporate Cult* it did make sense. Feelings were desensitized.

I persistently and assertively asked over and over for specific examples about why I did not fit in and why my appearance had anything to do with this. No matter how hard I tried, I was simply not given specific feedback. I also knew I was not a protected class under Title VII. I was told that it was my style, and that she could not comment about my performance. She said she did not really understand what I did as an issues manager doing futures research, so she did not feel that my performance was the issue. I was the one using logic and it did not work.

Although this sounds, and is, dysfunctional, within this ill system, it makes sense. I was never given direction, nor monitored, nor appraised so how could my performance be an issue? My function was not understood by many and therefore unmonitored, so she said. She suggested that I go to my vice president upon his return and request a transfer. I was quite confused with this feedback and didn't know if this woman was trying to do me a favor in my best interest or if she was looking out for her own best interest. Perhaps she was trying to project her discomfort with me to the vice president, whom I did not trust.

I reflected upon my last and only performance review with him. I received an average rating and was unable to question why because we had done a peer ranking and I was told that he could not answer for my peers. When I discussed the fact that few of them knew or understood my function he told me that it was my responsibility to educate them. I had mixed feelings about that. He then proceeded to advance with a series of very specific questions about how the department was being run and was allegedly seeking input from everyone in the group and wanted to use the performance review as a forum for discussing these policies and procedures.

I made a big mistake. I told him the truth. I must say that I did so professionally and politely, but I did in fact tell the truth about what I saw and how I felt things could operate with less stress and less chaos. I made the foolish assumption that since he asked for the information, he was truly interested in improving the work environment. I then felt that this was not an unrealistic assumption to make. It is actually pretty logical. I apparently wanted to keep believing that somebody would come along and clean up the *Corporate Cult*, just like magic, the same way many of us believe that we shall clean up our lives without effort, responsibility, discipline, and self honor. The tendency for all of us is to want to believe that all will be straightened out and that justice will reign and we shall live happily ever after. At the closure of our meeting he turned to me and said, "Your best quality is your complete candor." I realize now that he meant my "best quality" for his own purposes.

The meeting left me curious as to why the vice president approached me as he did. In this supposedly "open minded" group, why wouldn't a peer give me direct feedback in an adult, professional manner? Instead, someone allegedly went to him behind my back. The department was what I call, "In the think," and I realized that the possibility of me even tracking down any truth on this issue would be slim.

After some confrontations with a few selected peers in my group, I received no relevant information and did not want to generate energy toward this issue. To this day I am still not really sure what took place. Weeks later someone whom I regarded as a nice guy and a real family man who had clearly joined the *Corporate Cult* for job security did confide in me who had gone over my head complaining. As it turns out, it was someone whom I trusted in the group. Someone who in private expressed great empathy for my frustrations and yet in public was able to portray a much stronger cult commitment than I. His disloyalty hurt and surprised me. It was least expected. On another level I almost believed that he respected me so much that he hoped I would become unhappy and leave because he knew I was being destroyed.

When the vice president finally did come back from his vacation, I questioned him about the incident, which had occupied a great deal of my time. He responded with, "Oh that, it's nothing." Situations such as this caused my reality to be challenged regularly on so many levels. Did they just want me to act like a "crazy female"? Did I fulfill their expectations? One cannot function in a dysfunctional system without recognizing it for what it is. You see, I still clung to the hope that this system knew more than I did. I wanted to desperately believe that it was fair and that it would give me the answers about what to do. I still had belief in authority and even some respect. Had I accepted the dysfunction and refused to give it the power, I would have been much more peaceful and powerful. I continued to do my job and kept a very low profile.

A few weeks later, my boss called me into her office. At that time a rampant rumor was confirmed. She informed me that Harvard MBA graduates were being hired into the company and that most of "us," meaning my peers, would need to rotate out of the department as soon as possible. These individuals were being hired to do the same work we had been doing. We would be outplaced, misplaced, and they would be brought in to fill in behind us at a higher pay scale. It sounded so incredibly discriminatory that I was shocked. I have immense respect for Harvard graduates, however, I have immense respect for graduates of numerous other fine programs and I felt that I was one of them. I felt that my peers had exquisite training. At least half of them had M.A.s, two had Ph.D.s and I was working on a Ph.D. and had completed my M.A.

years ago. We also had some familiarity with the products. New blood and fresh ideas are good; however, the issue of balance again enters the scenario, or should have.

Management just didn't seem to be able to understand that there didn't need to be a duality, all Harvard MBAs versus no Harvard MBAs. This change had been rumored for some time and it was tough to manage. After all, we were only human and had worked, in our own way, to attain a certain level, and suddenly no job security. None of the upper management had a Harvard MBA and some didn't have M.A.s. My director had a B.A. in secondary education. She was probably one of the most competent, when it came to subject matter and working the business. The situation became one huge irony.

We were told that we would be expected to train these individuals and to a certain extent, befriend them. There was an actual series of orientation days that took place. Several candidates came to the company and were interviewed and then "taken around" by us, the people. Sometimes it is just hard to put our human nature aside and work out of total altruism, but I must say that I gave my work group an A+ for this. People were as kind and informative as possible. I think that we all knew that if we were rude to these candidates, it would serve no purpose, except to make us look small. They could very well be our bosses soon, too, and we knew that as well. There was no need to kill the messenger. In some ways I could empathize with them because during my assignment in human resources, I often felt discriminated against due to my advanced education. After all of the "personal" mind games which I had experienced and survived, it seemed so bittersweet that my education would end up being my weak point. It is a good lesson to always know that no matter what, there is always someone smarter, someone less bright, someone more qualified, and someone less qualified. Well, as it were, we all felt quite dispensable.

During this time of corporate "house cleaning," *having* a "sponsor" or mentor was crucial to survival in the *Corporate Cult* and race. I particularly remember the story of a "yes man." Everyone liked and respected him. He also happened to be quite a dedicated family man. He was asked to pursue a M.A. in an evening program with the hopes that he could then stay in the department. He had strong ties to the departmental leaders. He refused to attempt a further degree because it would take away time from his family. I respected this man a lot more when he told me this story. It must have been a hard decision for him. In my opinion, he only portrayed a yes man because he needed a secure income for his family.

I knew yet another man who had a M.A. and was demoted because at one point in a meeting with his boss he expressed a desire to spend more time with his family. I point these cases out to demonstrate that although women and minorities frequently and regularly get the "shaft," there are indeed plenty of white males who suffer when they refuse to conform and drink the Koolaid. These are the real men—strong enough to give their families priority status.

As this situation transpired, some of the very best and more innovative individuals left the company. It was no coincidence that two of them were highly motivated, aggressive white females, one with a Ph.D. and one with a MBA from an outstanding university in the Midwest. Although I did not always see eye to eye with these employees, they sometimes encouraged awareness and provoked thought.

I had always suspected that this department in particular was very prejudiced. We had, at the time, only one minority employee; an ingenious black male who also left at this time to go into business for himself. It seemed as though a group was selected to be the hit list and the list was hit. One by one, everyone on the list was given some "incentive" to leave. It could be a horrible appraisal, a very undesirable job, whatever. The individuals being driven out all had certain qualities of heightened awareness and generally expressed their nonconforming views at various levels. It didn't take me long, although in my great density, it took longer than it would now or "should have," to realize that I was on the hit list.

I didn't want to believe that this was happening. How could it? I had always done the right thing and I had come to work on time and rarely took sick days. I worked late and on weekends. So much for ethics and morality. So much for hard work, and apple pie with American cheese on top. The "good old boys network" was doing a lot of shuffling to find ways to take care of the boys who had paid their private dues. Many transfers occurred. I sat and watched while several of my peers were transferred into positions for which I was much more qualified due to education and experience. When would I get it through my head that in this game, experience and credentials were irrelevant?

My boss told me that she didn't know how long she could protect me. The entire happening was so strange because I had such mixed feelings. Who would want to be a part of the situation and who would want to stay working with these people? A huge part of me had so many other plans and ideas and inspirations to pursue but along with them came fear and misery. This eight and one-half year corporate marriage had gone bad. I was being cheated and I was being abused. My long-term plan had been to complete my Ph.D. which was about two years away and to then leave the company unless I found that I was happy.

The reorganization and intervention caused me to reevaluate the plan. I decided to not act in a rash manner and began looking for another assignment inside the company. I was close to being vested and did not want to give this up after years of hard work and dedication. My boss was helpful but I could always noticeably see her playing both sides of the fence. In a weak moment, she told me that I was a pain and got in her way. If she didn't have to worry about transferring me, she could spend more time politicking. I know that she was torn because she felt that there was injustice, although she wasn't really sad at the thought of me leaving.

I knew that the company's contract with the union was coming to a close and since I had a graduate degree in labor and industrial relations, I felt that I had, or should have had, a good crack at getting the opening in the labor relations department as a member of the team. It was a temporary assignment but I felt that I could do my best and then possibly be offered a full-time assignment in this department. It was also a "level-less assignment," meaning that whoever took it would keep their current salary grade, no promotions and no demotions. That sounded fair to me so I scheduled myself for an interview.

My interview was with an employee from the labor relations department who was two salary grades below me and who had only been with the company for about a year. He was supposed to be the leader of one of the bargaining teams. There were three. I thought that the arrangement was a little different but I figured that he must be awfully good at what he did to be charged with such an assignment. (Sometimes my density was unyielding.)

I had the interview and it seemed fine. He didn't ask me many questions, I had to initiate most of the conversation. I needed a transfer and I genuinely felt that the job would be an exciting challenge. He informed me that since pieces of the bargaining strategy were in place, I would be doing research, doing a lot of note taking and documentation, but he assured me that, if "chosen for the job," I would surely be a big asset to the department with my fine credentials.

There was another employee, a white male, working in the department who had the same graduate degree as did I and was highly regarded. A week passed and I heard nothing. I called the person who interviewed me and he told me that he was just too busy to make a decision or sit down and discuss the opening with his boss. I accepted this, I had no choice.

A week later at 11:30 p.m., my boss phoned me at home and said, "I have wonderful news. I just got done talking to the director of labor relations and I begged him to give you the temporary assignment." She then explained that they had an excellent rapport and that she could "do this type of thing with him." I quietly sat in silence and in awe while she came back with, "I can't believe how ungrateful you are, you certainly are unappreciative." Her comments at 11:30 p.m. were at the very best upsetting. I patiently thanked her and hung up the phone.

Survival and Transformation Strategies

1. **Be aware of your emotional IQ and try to strengthen it with keen awareness of yourself and others.** If you don't know much about emotional IQ, look it up on the internet or purchase a book about it. There are many on the market. There are even surveys or self-profiles that you can take to improve your emotional intelligence. This will help you survive by giving you a sense of peace, and others will automatically feel more at ease with you, as your emotional IQ expands. As it expands, bioenergetically, the more space you take up. Taking up space in a positive way is a good thing. This can only help you. Start by reframing negative cliches. Instead of saying, "Killing two birds with one stone," say, "Planting two trees with one seed."

2. **Get out of the *think* and examine what memes you might have that are holding you back on the job, and in life.** Memes are thought patterns that affix themselves to our psyche. We get them each day and give them out. Our strongest memes are likely a part of our DNA. Explore your consciousness so that you know what your hot buttons are. If you know them, or if you know your memes, you can reframe them. Or, you can protect them. If you are not conscious in a competent way, you may be caught off guard with attacks on your belief system. These memes can be

macro concepts in which you believe, or they can be very personal and specific.

3. **Explore your shadows.** Are you *a dear one*, a *knight*, a *monarch*, or *heyoka?* Likely, you have all four of these figures with you in some way. If you are in perfect balance, you will likely understand all four of them, and how they manifest in you. The dear one is the peace keeper and people person. The knight can be a hero and is brave and at times, fearless. The monarch can be arrogant and demanding. The heyoka is a trickster. The heyoka teaches like a fox—and a wise one. All figures can be positive or negative, just as a cat can sit quietly sleeping and purring on your lap, just after it returns from killing innocent prey. Know who you are and who your adversaries are. Learn their styles. Know your patterns and tendencies.

Personal Journaling

CHAPTER FIVE
Getting To Yes?

The next day the director of labor relations called me into his office and asked me why my boss was so incredibly desperate to get rid of me. Luckily, I was able to quickly collect my thoughts to form an appropriate response to an inappropriate question; "Why, because I have always wanted to sit at a bargaining table and she is concerned with my career goals and best interest." It is hard to look in the mirror after telling these types of lies, at least for me. It reminds me of the Dudley Moore movie, *Crazy People* in which everyone told the truth. In the movie, the truth was awarded positive consequences, unlike the movie *Liar, Liar*. I wonder what would have happened if I had responded, "I wish I knew. I think she is being pressured to transfer me out of the department because she believes that the vice president doesn't like me and doesn't feel that I fit the corporate mold." At the time, this response was not even a remote option for me.

The director of labor relations thought he was very handsome, but was indeed pompous, arrogant, crude, and the epitome of a chauvinist. He used profanity regularly. He liked to scream and shout. He would often make phone calls while one was having conversation with him and was in mid-sentence. He seemed to have little ability to concentrate. His attention was always scattered as if he lived only in his own vacuum. He often engaged in monologue and dialogue with himself. I later found that he had come from another large company and with him he brought the person who interviewed me and who reported to him. I knew that I could never join this boy's club. He had also gone to my alma mater and was closely bonded with the other individual who attended my program.

Each day was filled with *Playboy* jokes, discussion of centerfolds, descriptions of the female anatomy, excessive swearing, and very offensive and personal sexual harassment. I remained starry eyed and enthusiastic for about one month, until my blinders and denial stopped working completely. If I was not being harassed, somebody else was, or I could overhear discussions which should have been private or should have not existed. A frequent topic was the amount and type of sex they had the night before and the details of it.

I had foolishly vowed to myself to stick this out. I believed a formal complaint would have taken me down and out even faster. Before I left my last assignment, my boss said to me, "You had better not ruin this; I stuck my neck out for you and you had better not make me look like a fool." In addition, I found that when the labor relations director was so aggressively coaxed by my boss to hire me, he did some interrogation on his own and talked with my old boss in human resources. Apparently he did not give any specific comments about me or my performance but said, "Oh, whoopie, my God, you hired her!" This information was presented to me by the head of the bargaining team, who for all practical purposes was my boss, even though I was to officially report to the director because of my higher salary grade. The head of the team told me that one of the reasons they wanted me was that they disliked the human resources director and figured that if he didn't like me, I must be great. The dysfunctional thinking and negative self-esteem messages were layered and enmeshed so that everyone gave and received negative energy. The lies, the injustice, and the ironies just got thicker and thicker and thicker.

During that first month, I forced myself to smile a lot and be very resilient. I consciously tried to screen out the offensive comments and actions. It became particularly embarrassing when we were expected to come in and work each and every weekend full time. The reason why this became unbearable was that there was ridicule if you did not wear shorts, since it was the hot summer. If you did, there was a detailed analysis of your legs. It was not unusual to walk by the director's office and hear him shouting through a closed door, "Fu** you, you son of a *itch!" It was impossible for me to regard this man with respect or as a role model. This man had no discretion. During meetings, a secretary would walk out of the room and he would comment on her body. Two favorites were, "Christ, she's got big tits," or "Her ass jiggles too much." This lewd behavior was a disgrace to the company, the profession, and even the *Corporate Cult*.

There were other women in the department with whom I gained alliances and they all clearly warned me. I was told that the department was for the boys and that if I rocked the boat, I would be out. Out began to look better and better.

Eventually the actual bargaining sessions began and the team moved into a local hotel. The head of the bargaining team was moved into a suite. There were two other members of the team on the company side and they were both white males who were on rotational assignments from other departments, lending their "expertise" to the table. Both were clearly "of the good old boys network." One was only a facade cult member, clinging to the cult only when his job security was an issue. In his personal life, he was not an unconscious conformist. Each of these men were lodged in regular hotel rooms. I was also put into a regular hotel room, however, there were a few differences. The first difference was that in my room went the computer.

Along with the computer came a modem and a printer, extra phones and additional paraphernalia. I felt a little closed-in and claustrophobic. I had seen how lavishly and irresponsibly the "upper levels" of the department showered themselves with perks and amenities, particularly when traveling. The comparison was way out of sync. I tried to calm myself down and affirm that this was just part of the job. Later I found out that it was not just part of the job. For starters, there were other states participating in bargaining agreements and as I spoke with my counterparts at the other bargaining tables at out-of-state locations, I was consistently informed that it was very unusual that my room would house the computer since the team head was given a suite for that very reason. I let it go, because I felt I may be able to work more privately in my own room but that was a big misconception.

Other members of the team were given keys to my room so that I had little or no privacy day and night. In addition to this, two of the team members chain-smoked and this meant that I usually had a smoke-filled room. Because the special phone lines and computers were in my room, all of the after hours meetings were held in my room. I began to nicely, politely and finally aggressively persist that there be no smoking in my room and I got laughs coupled with sarcastic jokes.

Frequently I would hear, "Oh that's right, *you* have that smoking problem," which would effectively frustrate me. It seemed bad enough that all day and often long into the evening I would sit at the hotel (conference room) table and inhale their seemingly endless cigarette smoke. One evening the director called on the bargaining hotline and I just happened to be in the room alone. I very casually expressed my concerns to him regarding room privacy and cigarette smoke. I was fervently informed that bargaining was a tense situation and that if I chose not to be a team player, I would get kicked out. "There is no room for trouble makers," is how he put it. I foolishly followed that direct and repressive command and went on trying to function in a dysfunctional situation. A few members of the union smoked and they were much more respectful and accommodating, often leaving the room when lighting up. In this way and others, they truly appeared to bargain in good faith and made the experience worthwhile.

I completely understand and appreciate vantage points and bargaining and although I had never before worked with a union, I had been in bargaining situations often. My team, I am sorry to say, demonstrated a lack of integrity on most counts and very weak ethical standards. Labor relations agreements encompass far more than signed contracts. They encompass many intangible attributes and qualities, which are critical and mandatory for a relationship of truth, compromise, flexibility, and progress to occur. They include respect, dignity, honor, sensitivity, empathy, and especially integrity.

The global economy of the 21st century dictates this type of relationship and permits no alternatives if economic survival is to endure.

They sometimes regarded the union as a joke and I could see no way that there could ever be a win-win situation or even an equitable agreement without basic human respect and dignity. Maybe this attitude is truly obsolete, idealistic and just a fantasy, but it is one that I was not willing to concede.

Ironically, the bargaining team members were all commanded to read the book, *Getting to Yes*, which prompted very high ideals due to the high moral standard it reflected. If we were not going to operate this way, why did we bother to read it, and why all the mixed messages? For whose benefit was this mockery? The *Corporate Cult* seems fond of exercises, which validate the facade.

One evening my fiance, Kevin, came to the hotel to take me to dinner. I knew that it was going to be an earlier night, so I made the date. When he walked into my room I could see the look of intense disgust move across his face. He later told me that although I had shared my situation with him, he believed that I must have been exaggerating. When he saw my room with three men comfortably perched there, a computer next to my bed, paper all over, filled ash trays and a thick cloud of old stale smoke, empty beer bottles, junk food and candy wrappers; he knew it was all very true. Worst of all were the crude commentaries. He was amazed that I could survive such an episode in masochism. They watched my TV. They listened to my radio. A few times I simply told everyone to get out, but then they played me to be the "bitchy woman . . . on the rag." Most typically I was told to be like a man if I wanted to do a man's job.

When Kevin and I came back from dinner, we tried to sit quietly in peace and after fifteen minutes, there were men flying in and out of my room allegedly looking for papers. Kevin left. I began making occasional drives home very late at night. It was about a half hour drive so I could have commuted more, but I was reprimanded when it was discovered that I had made a few trips home.

Since I was engaged, I regularly heard a stream of marital jokes, pieces of advice, reasons why not to marry, and the like. I received graphic details on the sleeping habits and sexual activities of married couples. At the time, like many women in the work place, it was hard for me to draw the line and exert assertive behavior. I was falling into the duality role syndrome of being a hysterical woman or a nice Pollyanna. To make matters worse, when I had tried to assert my position gently and firmly, I was told that I was a trouble maker and that there was no room for that kind. My simple human rights and needs were violated, discarded and grossly minimized.

I remember the *Corporate Cult* taking away one's knowingness and intuition. This would have been the time to quit, but so many friends and family told me not to give up my job for these characters. This is common advice we hear from our friends and loved ones who may not truly see for themselves the soul-murder and power stripping that goes on. Getting another job is far easier than getting another self. The levels of humiliation, which I experienced, were so deep that I remember leaving my own room when it was filled with men, so that I could use a lobby restroom in privacy. During certain times of the month I really needed to do this, which is no more than taking care of my basic human needs.

One afternoon the union and management went out to lunch together at an Italian restaurant and I ordered a Cajun dish. Shortly after arriving back to the hotel my eyes turned bloodshot and I felt very weak and hot. I broke out in welts and could not stand or walk. I had eaten Cajun food before and had never experienced any reaction, let alone such an extreme one. I was bedridden for about a day and, of course, was stuck in my room, with everyone right there. As the evening grew, they finally left. When I got sick everyone seemed honestly nice and concerned but I just wanted to be alone. I just wanted to be sick in private. I did not want to go on display and become the center of more lewd and crass jokes, which is just what happened. Some of their concern was well-intentioned, but still offensive.

I also broke a toe while being on the bargaining team. This occurred in a freak accident and I now believe that my psyche and body were simply looking for ways for me to escape this toxic team.

The head of the bargaining team had few interpersonal skills to pull out of his bag of tricks. I loathed his prejudice and inability to bargain effectively and felt very sorry for him. I decided that the big picture goal had to be more important than my personal goal and ego. This is dysfunctional reasoning especially when nobody else even comes close to feeling this way.

The union had come to me and asked if our team leader had been trained to act as he did, was he doing it on purpose, was he at all aware of what bargaining in good faith meant? This was a very sad scene because union and management, at least the table at which I sat, did not really have any unresolvable conflicts. The company had plenty to give and the union was quite reasonable. Instead, the conflicts of bargaining dealt with attitudes and styles.

I understand that to a degree persistence, abruptness, and keeping your hand hidden are necessary and customary, but there is dirty dealing and there is good faith bargaining. I felt so awkward. I was hired to be on management's side and presented such a front, however, in my heart I recognized that the union was acting in good faith. Their behavior was more professional, more humane, more honest and certainly concerned with real life critical issues, such as supporting their families. The head of the union team was an extremely competent and well-read, black female who had years of experience. The entire team represented diversity.

One night I sat in my room realizing that the contract would be up in just a few days. I assessed the situation and realized that a strike was bound to occur if the team leader did not come down to earth and off of his pedestal. By now, all other members of my team had noticed his persistent aloofness and his inflexibility. We discussed it, but they were much less committed than I to get involved or become "trouble makers." They had long-time careers at stake and this team leader, "the fair haired, golden boy" had perceived power. However, I feel that their opinions and our joint effort could have outweighed this "golden boy's" delusion, even though his boss, the director, made it clear that he gave the team leader blind support. As usual, I took my so-called trouble maker identity and plunged ahead. The company did not want to strike. I called his suite and asked if I could speak with him in person. He agreed. I went to his suite and knocked on the door. Knowing his mind, he probably thought that I had other intentions.

I had my dialogue all planned out. I realized that this guy was certainly not going to become altruistic overnight, so I made a plan to appeal to his already overindulged ego. The interesting nuance is that all that I said was very true. I approached him as though I was approaching a customer to whom I wanted to sell a product or concept. I reviewed the company's goals. I accentuated the concept of how vital successful bargaining was in order for his career to shine and that he could do so by signing the contract on time. I reviewed with him many remaining issues and discussed his behavior at the table. Then I gave him outs, such as telling him that perhaps he was so over worked and so consumed with the process that he was unable to be as objective as usual about his perspective and perceptions.

I was very glad that I chose to speak with him because somehow it was a moment of truth, like a piece out of a well-acted stage scene. When an actor does a scene and suddenly realizes that he or she is the scene, there is a certain fulfillment and totality. It is a high. It is like an emotional peak. This is what I experienced when I spoke with this man. I could actually feel the energy in the room switch and I became in control. He, for the first time, listened intently with absolute eye contact. I could see that although there were many veils of ignorance between us, we had connected on this issue and he knew that I was right. He thanked me in what felt and appeared to be a very sincere fashion and said no more. I left. The contract was settled the following day. That's the good news.

The bad news is that his behavior toward me got worse and worse. He became ruder, this time he tried avoiding me, as though he were ashamed and refused to acknowledge any conversation or my presence. That mellowed after a few days and things got "back to normal" which was still crude and uncomfortable, but at least it was familiar. We all moved out of the hotel and back to the office.

We signed the contract and I must say that I was at an all time high. I never dreamed that it would make me feel so happy, nor had I realized how truly connected I had been to the bargaining experience. I felt so proud and accomplished to have played a part on the team. I remember calling Kevin, late at night, actually awakening him from a deep sleep to tell him of the settlement. He was astonished by my exuberant enthusiasm. I remember him questioning me about how I could be so elated after all that they had put me through. Somehow, I managed to thrive on the energy of accomplishment.

Back at the office it was only a week or so until I began to realize that I would have to find another permanent assignment and I wondered if I could stay in the labor department. Concurrently, there was a strike at one of our out-of-state locations, and a sign-up sheet was circulated for strike duty. I signed up and was sent out of state for about five weeks. One day I received a call from the "golden boy" and he requested that I return from strike duty to assist in the final preparation on the new contract. Although I had telephoned my office regularly, there had been no imminent reason for me to return. When I received word of being needed back at headquarters, I left that day. When I came back, I was wondering if there would be an assignment awaiting me in labor relations. I was confident that I had "paid my dues" and had not been the "trouble maker." I was told that I had to go back to corporate planning and development.

This was most frustrating for many reasons, but especially because before I had gone on strike duty, I was given a so-called "career plan form" by the director of labor relations. He told a group of us that since we had "come through for him" he would see that we got taken care of. Somehow this made the trials and the long summer months spent over bargaining seem worthwhile. I thought that finally I would receive retribution for my hard work. I secretly felt relieved that "the system did work." I was satisfied that I had not made "waves," while being on the bargaining team.

This was not the case. When I questioned being reassigned back to corporate planning, I was not really given an answer. The former team head could not even look me in the eyes when he delivered the news. This is probably because he had indeed entertained and initiated many blundering comments about corporate planning throughout the summer months. I heard endless talk and scorn aimed at my boss, the director of development, and her boss, the vice president of corporate planning and development.

I decided to go to the director of labor relations and ask him if he could assist me in finding a suitable transfer. He immediately dismissed me and asked why I was coming to him. I explained that he had been my temporary boss, so to speak, and that my salary had been coming out of his department for months. He responded by saying that there were head count problems and that he couldn't help me, and to please get the hell out of his office so that he could work. I left his office and realized that I had few choices.

When my female boss, the director of development, had sent me to labor relations, she had clearly wanted it to be a one way transfer with no rotating back. Now I had to deal with her. I moved back to corporate planning and my boss asked me, "What in the world are you doing back here? I told you not to get into any trouble because then I wouldn't be able to help you." She inquired about my experience in labor relations and I told her the highlights in truth. She appeared to be very anxious as she confided in me that she had heard talk of this type of awful behavior and had also witnessed it herself. I was told that I approached my work professionally and with enthusiasm. I was also told that I was very ingenious in terms of creative ways to get information and that my interpersonal skills were superior. In fact, the entire department attended media training and my exemplary performance in front of the camera and my comfort with responding to prying questions on the spot had actually circulated back to my boss.

We agreed on a strategy. The strategy was to get me a very good ranking, and thereby, she would be able to represent me well enough to support my efforts in finding a "suitable transfer." She felt that since, due to a number of variables, one being that my function of future research was being phased out, it would be difficult for her to give me a ranking above average. We felt that since I expected a high ranking from my bargaining assignment, that there should be minimal difficulty in pursuing this option. My function was being phased out because the company did not have a temperament compatible with that of pro-activity. I actually initiated the phase-out because I could see my research was never reviewed.

I had spent countless hours on researching trends, analyzing them, preparing issue briefs, and documenting variables from the trends, which would directly impact the company, its shareholders, and the employees. After numerous attempts, the information was never questioned, it was ignored and never discussed or in some cases never read. There were documents, which took unbelievable amounts of time, clerical power, and expense to create, which were simply not utilized. Although I believed in the function and had seen it work effectively at the other division of the company in which I worked, I realized that my efforts were deemed as fruitless. Since this was how they were perceived, I saw no reason in perpetuating grandiosity and ego protection. I did this at a time when I still believed that justice would prevail and that the "good of the whole" was important.

Regardless of my intentions, the company was not yet ready or open to utilize or even synthesize the types of documents I prepared. At one point we hired my former boss, who had trained me in this area. She and I conducted a seminar within the department based on the premise that if people were more informed of the function and could truly brainstorm, they would get out of "group think," design creative options, understand and possibly get excited about the function.

We wanted to institute an environmental scanning committee, which would encourage company involvement. Even my peers could not relate to my efforts and my projects were given the name "stargazer" by my former male boss, which further provoked several jokes. Since the function was simply a waste of time at this company, I suggested and supported that it be discontinued until a later time where more open-minded management existed. Needless to say, my bosses supported this proposal and probably would have abolished it whether I suggested so or not. None of the Harvard graduates would be performing such analyses. I found it discouraging that I had been paid high wages to perform a function about which nobody cared. I was basically told by my boss and the vice president that they only supported the efforts of futures research initially, due to the fact that the chairman of the holding company had strongly believed in the function. So, I essentially served as a figurehead or a token.

In the meantime, labor relations was very slow in preparing any kind of an evaluation of my performance. During this time I was given token assignments and since my work area had been reassigned, I sat in a chair among the secretarial pool while I continued to make a fine salary. This was a lose-lose situation. They did not utilize my abilities and I felt underemployed.

A position opened in our parent company out of state. The opportunity was in the area of strategic research, including scanning, and was a few salary levels above mine. This would have been a promotion for me. I immediately completed the paperwork and took the forms to my vice president to sign. My immediate boss was out of town for a few weeks and there was a deadline for paperwork submission. When I approached him with the idea he grabbed the package out of my hand and said, "If you think I am going to sign this, you're crazy; get it out of here." I felt as though I was a mosquito who had landed on his arm. He gave me a figurative slap, nonetheless, a slap.

I had previously dealt with counterparts at the parent company and decided to take the initiative to call them on my own to get an extension for my paperwork. I found out that because there were surplus conditions at the parent and within other operations, it might be difficult for me to get a promotion. I did get an extension and was also told that I had basically been performing the job for which I applied, it just happened to be at a level higher at the parent organization. This encouraged me to continue my pursuit.

When my boss returned to the office, she signed my paperwork. It stated that I was qualified for promotion. She noted on the form that the assignment had to be a career move and that I could not serve as a rotational, nor would the company consider a buy back.

Within the system, it was quite common for HRM to transfer to jobs for "temporary" assignments, which could last even three to five years. I questioned how she could recommend me for a promotion slot at the parent company yet seemed unable to assist me in finding a transfer for me at my level within the company and location at which I worked. She told me that she knew that I could do the job at the parent, but that she would never recommend me for a promotion at my current location, nor would her boss approve it, and that she would have to beg him to sign the form. My career was on a chessboard. I was clearly in a pawn position and the opposition had my queen.

The vice president signed my paperwork, recommending me for the job, for the promotion. A few weeks later the division manager at the parent company telephoned me and he told me that I had not been selected for the job. He explained that there had been a district manager on surplus at the parent company who had done similar types of work and he was placed in the job.

Actually, I felt that their choice was quite ethical and felt great respect for the decision-makers. My dilemma remained the same. I decided to make some candid calls to some contacts, which I had at the parent company, and I attempted to moderately disclose what had transpired in my career. I received affirmation that the parent company was allegedly aware that this type of activity was taking place but was, at that time, not in a position to rectify things. I was somewhat disappointed about not being selected for the job but at the same time, I was relieved that I did not have to relocate. I was near the dissertation phase of my doctorate and had no desire to leave behind all of the hard work that I had invested at a local university. This also would have meant that Kevin and I would have been living in different cities, unless he changed jobs.

As I reflected back on my initial hiring into the company, as a part of the initial management development program, and reviewed my high marks, I felt as though my career had slipped through my hands. The worst of it was that I truly did not know why. There was nothing concrete on which to analyze it. There were no "bad" reviews, no suspensions, and no warnings. I wondered if maybe somehow I was just really misunderstanding the point of it all.

Paradoxically, I think that hiring into the "initial management development program" (IMDP) was one of the worst things that happened to me. From the program I knew no woman or minorities who had made it to the "top," yet we were all supposed to be "so good." In fact, even among the white males from my program, I can think of only one who made it to a job level above me. Overall, most levels of management resented the program. There always seemed to be a stigma associated with the IMDP. The general attitude expressed was that we never really paid our dues. Others seemed to feel that because of advanced education and certain character traits, which allowed us to score highly during assessment, we were given golden opportunities.

There was a white male IMDP associate with whom I stayed in somewhat regular contact and he experienced perils similar to mine, although they came about earlier in his career. He finally transferred to yet another division and seemed to surrender the ideals that we had been promised.

I finally received my evaluation from the labor department and I was very relieved . . . until I read it. The corporate ranking system which was employed by the company ranked employees on a scale from one to five. One was poor and unacceptable performance, while five was superior performance. Those of us having subordinates had been told that five would not be awarded. For every four awarded, there needed to be an equal number of ones and twos to balance out the rankings. Raises were not necessarily granted, regardless of one's ranking. Three was average.

As I read through my appraisal, I was stunned to find that I had been given a two. I telephoned one of the district managers who had been my peer on the bargaining team and then I went to see him. I showed him the appraisal and he said he couldn't believe it either. I finally started to realize that I could be sure of little, except for my own intuition and feelings. He suggested that I go to the district manager of labor relations, since he was officially my boss, although the appraisal was written by the bargaining team head, who remained two salary grades below me. According to my appraisal, my Achilles' heel was my clerical ability.

I went to my boss and she was angry when reading the appraisal, both with labor relations and at me for drawing her into the situation. She thought that possibly "golden boy" was afraid that I was more qualified and wanted to be sure that I never ended up being his boss. It all made sense, yet it made no sense at all. I asked her to give me some time to get the rating changed and she agreed.

First, I did contact the district manager of labor relations. He gave me five minutes of his time. He listened as I firmly stated my case. I brought reports that I had prepared, and my calendar, which had a thorough documentation of my involvement in bargaining. He looked at me and said, "I will be willing to change the rating to whatever the team leader says." He pulled the ultimate Pontius Pilate, leaving me absolutely no appeal process at all. He then refused to discuss it further. I contacted "golden boy" and he said that he could not fit me into his schedule for some time. When we did meet, I brought with me, a suggested appraisal that I had written, in which I outlined what I had accomplished on and for the team. I was prepared to bargain with him and I knew what that would be like.

We spent about four hours in a closed-door session going over each single task and project on which I had worked. I taped the conversation, although he did not know it. I did not want the reality to escape me. I wanted proof of what was happening. I used sales techniques and after each point I asked him for agreement or concurrence. At the close of our meeting it was clear to me that I had truly challenged his belief system. Because of the way I designed my forum and because of the real dialogue that transpired, I felt quite sure that he would meet me, at least half way. I could see *no* other logical outcome. He argued with almost each point I made. I conducted myself very professionally and treated him with respect, quite a personal challenge for me under the circumstances. He said he needed time to reevaluate my performance.

Simultaneous to these events, I received a letter which said,

Dear Diane:

Congratulations! Your dedication to excellence and personal sacrifice throughout the bargaining process has established the foundation for the continued success of the company.

Please accept the enclosed check in recognition and appreciation of your extraordinary contribution to this process.

Sincerely,

The president of the company and the six vice presidents signed the letter. I found the letter quite humorous since I had been told that my performance was a "mere two" or below average. Of course, they try to tell employees that a "two" rating doesn't really mean below average; "the company has such high standards that a 'two' is average." This was, of course, meaningless since none of the "cult clones" would ever consider a two rating acceptable for their purposes of climbing the ladder.

I took the letter and check to my boss and told her that I refused to accept them since they were totally inconsistent with my rating and somehow somebody was going to have to tell me the truth. I planned to stand by my principles. She advised me to keep the money and shut up about the letter—again not to be a troublemaker.

I took the check and letter to the director of labor relations ("rage man") and questioned him on the contradiction, which I held before him with all seven signatures and fresh ink. He explained to me, in his own troubled logic, that the letter meant nothing, nor did the check. It was a token and a standard procedure which went out to almost all who served on the bargaining teams. This did not clear up the matter for me at all. If I had done a bad job, then I deserved no letter of commendation and certainly no bonus check of appreciation! "Rage man" could not relate to my message. He again threw me out of his office and referred me to the person who had prepared my appraisal. I challenged him with the information that I was indeed two levels (in this level-free organization) above "golden boy," and although he may have had skills in certain areas, was it not possible that I could have been treated unfairly? He refused to address the issue and ordered me to leave.

I then decided to go to the vice president of human resources/labor relations division. I did not feel as though I could go to the director of human resources for obvious reasons; my former experiences with him. My boss had requested that I not go to her boss and only deal with her on this matter. I had agreed since she was most definitely the only person who genuinely demonstrated any cognizance of the happenings. In her own way, I also believed that she did not want to see this particular injustice. I made the choice to wait until "golden boy" made his final ranking decision before I scheduled a meeting with the vice president of labor relations and human resources. The *Corporate Cult* always recommends that one follow channels, but sometimes it is simply not practical, realistic, or smart.

A few days later I approached the head of the bargaining team again, "golden boy." I asked him for his final decision. With a vise grip on his ego, he handed me the same original appraisal and professed that all things considered, he decided to keep it the same. I asked how this could be possible when he agreed with me on so many issues. He simply told me that he decided that the areas in which I excelled were not very important ones. By this time, I was getting very clear on the fact that being right had little or no meaning. I also knew by then that logic was not a technique employed by any of the people gatekeeping this situation. I explained the conversation to my boss and she shared my frustration. Unfortunately her compassion was running out, since she felt a real need "to dump me," which she did not hesitate to express. I told her about the meeting that I wanted to have with the vice president of human resources/labor and she agreed that it was necessary and wanted to join me, but asked me to take a look at a few job possibilities before I decided to have that confrontation.

My former job in human resources had emerged. They had never filled the job as training and development manager since I had left the group. When she showed me the job description, we agreed that I was perfectly suited, in fact, ironically, I had written the job description before I left the job. It seemed somewhat safe to assume that I would be granted this position and that this would give me a lateral assignment, which I found acceptable. I did not even mind going back to work for the director of human resources. After what I had experienced, I felt I could go to fight in the Middle East.

So, I scheduled an interview for my former job. As it turned out, the director of human resources had decided that the training and development job would no longer report directly to him, but that it would report to a position that was a salary grade between director and manager. The man who now held this job had been one of my peers when I was training and development manager. In fact, he had been newly hired into the company and I can still remember being the only person in the group to take him out to lunch during his first week with the company.

When I walked into the interview, I realized that he was not in his office; he arrived thirty minutes later. He wanted to reschedule the interview, which I agreed to, but he warned me that he had decided to do some background checking on me since he wondered why my department wanted to get rid of me. Being in HRM, he was fully aware of the fact that most or many of the managers in my department were being transferred because of the new Harvard graduate MBA migration, so the investigating seemed personal. He told me that he had gone to labor and talked with a "few of the boys" and found that my performance was on the weak side. He then read from his yellow legal pad many comments which "the boys had made." I invited him to stop since it was pointless. I told him that I wanted an interview and that I would be back the day on which we had agreed. My boss was out of town that day, so I could not share with her, the tidbits of my little session.

I really did not know how to prepare myself for and protect myself in the upcoming interview, so I decided to again tape the session. This time I decided to be up front about the taping since I wanted to be sure to be able to play it back to someone in an appropriate forum, if need be. When I walked into the interview, I took out my tape recorder. His mouth dropped open to the floor and he exclaimed in a loud and vulgar voice, "What the hell do you think you're doing with that?" I told him, "I would like to tape this interview, if you don't mind." He began exhibiting tantrum-like behaviors. His office door was open and I looked outside of it and saw the clerical pool red with laughter and embarrassment for their boss. He said, "I demand you to get out of my office at once. I shall never consider you for this job, and I never want to deal with you again." I asked him to please get a hold of himself and calm down. He was shaking and trembling. Interesting reaction, I thought . . . just a bit paranoid.

I then began to engage myself in cult dialogue and proclaimed that I certainly would not tape the interview if he did not wish me to do so. And that the only reason that I even wanted to, was to observe my own interview and interpersonal skills so that I could perfect and improve them. I explained that it had been one of my goals for the year. Well, he believed me, regained composure and we went through the interview without the tape-recorder. Lose-lose, it was all the same. He asked me if I knew anything about the job for which he knew I had written the description. He had the nerve and audacity to verbally quiz me on the very description I had written. Of course, I played the game and behaved appropriately. It was times like this one that really made me feel that I was living in some other zone of reality. The entire situation was completely dysfunctional in all parts. In retrospect, I do not exclude myself from this statement.

Weeks went by and I did not hear any feedback about my interview. My boss intervened. She came back with information that the human resource department decided to grant me a job. It was a demotion, which reported to the manager of training and development, my former job. They had decided to hire an outsider to fill the spot; a new white male. I turned down the job, although my boss tried to talk me into taking it.

This occurred about the same week that we had our final bargaining wrap-up gala. All the vice presidents were there, as was the president of the company. Those of us who had participated in bargaining were given plaques and photos to "honor our superior performances." It was at this meeting that I asked the vice president of labor relations and human resources to please expect a call from me the next day to schedule a meeting. As I looked around the dinner table at the banquet, I took a good, hard honest inventory of the people sitting around me. Most had grimaces that could only be removed surgically. They were not people whom I admired. They were not people whom I particularly liked. They were people who could teach me lessons.

Yes, I had learned just about all that I needed in order to take the next step. At this banquet I basically came to grips with the fact that I would leave. There was nothing to fight for but dignity and justice. The more I fought, the less dignity I had and the more illusive justice became. Any money that they gave me felt like it had come from some cheap trick that I had performed by bequeathing my soul. I had been raped emotionally, intellectually, and spiritually. I had prostituted my values, my beliefs, and my person. How could I have let it happen?

For the sake of formality, I did indeed attend a meeting with my boss and the vice president of labor relations and human resources and it was much like all other meetings. He knew very little about company policy and my boss had to aggressively inform him of the details. He had at most, slim knowledge about his staff and who worked for him. In the end, he said it was just too bad that things happened as they did.

After the meeting my boss and I discussed other possibilities within the company. The next day I told her that I wanted to leave at the end of the year, which was just a month away. I had always wanted to someday own my own business, possibly a franchise, and I had done quite a bit of research on companies that had been of interest to me.

In the next few weeks I signed franchise papers and gave my notice. I was not the only woman within my group to leave the ranks of this particular company. Independent, self-starting and intelligent women had left. Within the same timeframe, a female attorney left. She had worked long and hard hours. When a legal vice president spot opened, she was passed over, and an outside male counsel was hired. He left after a few months.

Before he left he told me that "the management of the company did not operate in accordance with his way of doing business" and he did not feel that it was a good match. I very much respected this man and was not surprised to find that he did not fit in.

These stories are not uncommon. On some level, all of the characters tried to play the *Corporate Cult* game. I also tried. It is possible to survive and transform your career in *Corporate America*, with greater consciousness and other survival skills. It takes some time, effort and work.

As for our losses and gains, we have seen how often they are inextricably mixed. There is plenty we have to give up in order to grow. For we cannot deeply love anything without becoming vulnerable to loss. And we cannot become separate people, responsible people, connected people, reflective people without some losing and leaving and letting go.

Judith Viorst

Positive Memories

During these eight and one-half years, I was able to make four very special friendships with women who became my friends and have turned out to be very special in my life. One friend was hired the same day and we were able to share many of the same experiences and insights, though we were at different phases of life. What was especially affirming is that we were able to validate the information around us. (For a short time I was her boss.) This in no way means that we found answers, but sometimes we did. Mainly, we provided a lot of coping support for one another. She never sold her soul. We are still friends.

The second friendship that I made was with a woman who hired into my work location after I started. She also had a unique and impressive background, and brought a fresh perspective, much of which deviated from that of the cult. She left the company a few years before I did and has had a successful track of consulting positions. (The three of us were able to share frustrations and infrequent triumphs, and sometimes, we still do.) This woman lives less than a mile from me, and we are in regular contact.

After about four years with the company, I developed an enduring friendship with the woman who was, at the time, the secretary to my boss. This in and of itself went against the grain of corporate protocol in some work groups because of the "class conscious" network. This woman was ultimately promoted through the ranks of management until she left the company to take another spot at another corporation out of state. We have only infrequent contact.

The fourth friendship I encountered was with a free-lance writer who became one of my employees and stayed with the company after I left until she was "forced out" by yet another incompetent division for which I had never worked. The manager who ultimately caused her to leave had a history of sexually harassing female employees. She now works for the EPA, and is quite happy. We have regular contact.

The relationships were gifts. They are diamonds in a coal mine and I thank God for bringing them to me. They help nurture and protect my self-esteem.

Through the years, I actually had some fantastic mentors. My naivete was a gift and a curse at the same time. Today, all the players are gone and this company has merged with another company.

Since this experience, I have worked in academia, non-profit, and *Corporate America*. I did not want to return to *Corporate America*, but one of my life mentors advised me to go back and "teach." When I returned, using my own strategies, I had a very different experience. It was positive, but I realized I would never like the confinement I felt.

Survival and Transformation Strategies

1. **Get an attorney.** Find one even if you do not think you need one. This is the perfect time to leisurely recruit legal counsel. So many of us wait until we become backed into a corner and then frantically contact any attorney. Look around and interview a few. If you were pregnant, you would not wait until delivery time to find a doctor. When you are employed and involved in a career, you shouldn't wait until a climatic or critical point to find proper legal counsel. A good attorney, whom you trust, can be an invaluable ally. Taking this step will help you feel protected and give you the courage to prevent yourself from getting backed into a corner.

2. **Document your career and keep this document in a safe place.** Documentation serves many purposes. It is not merely a defensive exercise. Through the process of documentation, you are forced to think through what has happened and perhaps see the situation in new light. You

may have misperceived or have been overreacting. Of course, your documentation may avidly affirm that which left you unsettled to begin with. In a private way, without sharing your business, it can also allow you to objectively see your patterns or hate, and inspire you to initiate changes in yourself.

3. **Don't depend on logic to help you survive.** I am not suggesting that logic be discarded, but don't rely on it, for at times it is simply not available. Forcing logic into an illogical situation based in politics, emotions, favoritism or discrimination will only drive you mad and arouse frustration. After gentle probing or observation, accept what happens but vent through your documentation. Know that if need be, you have legal counsel.

Personal Journaling

CHAPTER SIX

"I'll See You in My Dreams"

The elements of virtue are: Justice, Courage, Temperance, Wisdom, Magnificence, Magnanimity, Liberality, Gentleness, Prudence.

Lane Cooper, *The Rhetoric of Aristotle*

During periods of career tension I experienced a number of dreams, both revealing and gripping. At the time, I believed what Freud said about dreams, referring to them as the manifestations of one's fears and fantasies. Although I still believe that fears and fantasies do indeed contribute to your dreams, I think that by interpreting them, one can learn about subconscious needs. It is important to review them in some way by writing them down or explaining the highlights into a recorder. This allows you the opportunity to later go back and see what connections these dreams might have to your life.

The most vivid dream, which I wrote down, but will never forget, is a very scary one that represented my situation in the *Corporate Cult*. There were two of me in the dream, one of me was ill and in a hospital room with a doctor while the other, "the healthy me," visited. I experienced the dream through this "healthy me." My sick or "unhealthy" side was unconscious when I came to visit and the doctors reassured me that she would be just fine. They shuffled me out of the room against my better judgment. In the dream I did not trust the doctors or people who were around me. The people around me were basically faceless individuals who I felt were somehow my peers. I remember not wanting to leave my other self with the doctors and fearing what they would do to her, but everyone was so calm and controlled. I knew that if I protested, there would be a scene and that it would be "my fault."

Somehow I ended up in my backyard and I had a terrible feeling of panic rush through my bones. I looked up and saw a very dear friend, someone who had taught me a great deal, but her face looked ominous. She looked me in the eye with a penetrating stare and told me that they had killed her, she was dead. She was referring to my other self, the one I had left on the table. The doctors inside had killed my other self. She had been injected with poison. Then as I turned my head to weep, I saw a huge serpent, many feet long and quite wide. He had a big grin on his face as he encircled my home and my yard. I could not escape. He looked so powerful and omnipotent. I frantically cried and cried; then my friend took my arm and told me to have a seat.

Although this dream occurred years ago, it still sends chills up and down my spine. It was so vivid and so colorful, I shall never forget the leer on the serpent's face nor the striking colors on his back. They were vibrant, yet so subtle, they seemed to be camouflaged by the lovely natural shrubs and trees. Yet once I caught his gaze, his presence was boldly overpowering.

For me, this dream represented my internal struggle between having my own identity and operating in an ethical environment with people whom I respected versus succumbing to the cult. The fact that I had a part, which was sick and unconscious, represented the part of myself that I betrayed when I played the cult games and pretended not to observe them or understand their ramifications. Part of me was unconscious and wanted to remain so; the alternative was too frightening. In the dream they killed a part of me, as I knew they might, for I never trusted them and never wanted to stand up for my rights. I was too cowardly to withstand the scenes and accusations. An important part of the dream that is true for me, and for all of humanity, is that although they killed a part of me, they killed the weaker side. The illuminated self, the higher self was the one who survived. The higher self is the one who became enlightened by seeing the truth, the serpent.

Seeing the snake was terrifying, and as soon as I awoke, I ran to the window to see if there was in fact a huge reptile circling my house. The dream made me want to move, but of course I realized that the snake had nothing to do with my place of residence. Luckily, what I had was only a dream and an outstanding warning with a taste of my true subconscious.

In the dream, when my friend told me to have a seat, this was symbolic of her telling me to slow down and stop racing through life. It was also a way of telling me to take the time to sit quietly and reflect, ponder, meditate, call it what you like. For the longest time after I had the dream I loathed snakes. In the western world and in western religions, snakes are often regarded as an evil symbol.

Kevin and I traveled to New Mexico where I had the chance to pet a snake at an Albuquerque museum. Although I was not as brave as my husband and would not hold the snake, I did pet him. To me, this really symbolized the end of our turf war. He had actually come to me in my dream as a great friend or friendly enemy, giving warning and scaring me enough to realize that I needed to change my life. I also learned, after spending much time studying the Native American culture, that snakes represent the earth and fertility. I think that I needed to become more balanced on the earth by sticking both feet firmly on the ground and nurturing my fertile creative side, my yin, or female side.

I had many other dreams which were less vivid, but still very thought provoking. In one, I lost something and nobody would let me have it. I was again with a group of faceless peers at a type of outing and they all seemed to know where the lost object was. I was not even sure what I had lost. I went back to my hotel room and then I realized that somebody had stolen the object. In the dream, I then reflected back to when it might have been taken. The stolen object was, of course, my intuitive and creative self. It had just drifted out of my body, which had been seduced by the cult.

In another dream I was at work with a friend who also worked for the company and we saw that somebody was spying on our conversations and whereabouts. These two dreams represented to me how much I felt like an outsider and how afraid I was of having to hide who I really was, afraid that somebody would in fact steal my identity.

One dream consisted of a classic cliché, but was insightful nonetheless. In it I saw a small white elephant running around my office. He attended meetings and was clearly visible to me. I was naked and broken out in hives. When I pointed him out, nobody else could see him until he grew larger and larger. When he finally became full-size at two tons, a few began to acknowledge his presence while others still denied it. The elephant, of course, represented all of the problems contained within the cult norms that my work group refused to acknowledge or handle.

The frustration experienced in my dreams was not unlike the frustration I experienced in my career. So many times I witnessed experiences, that were almost impossible to comprehend. I became involved in situations that seemed unbelievable. This confusion and frustration had all been trapped in my psyche. This is what the hives were all about. The vision of myself naked represented my defenselessness and vulnerability. I felt exposed and unprotected.

Freudian Psychology Suggests?

An example of the difference between identity and identification might make the meaning of the two items clearer. When a person dreams that he is being chased by a lion, he ordinarily feels as though a real lion were chasing him. During a dream, the images are not distinguished from the real objects that they represent. They are identities. Consequently, a dreamer experiences the same emotion he would feel if the events of the dream were actually taking place.

Calvin S. Hall, *A Primer of Freudian Psychology*

I know that my dreams had powerful emotions from which to draw insight. I felt totally blocked at many times in my career and I dreamed of this as well. One dream was about my being stuck in a parking lot. No matter where I drove in my car, I was blocked and so frustrated. I could not get through no matter what I seemed to do. I then decided to get out of the car, so I left it and sneaked into a building. When I went through the front door, I noticed a huge reception room beyond the lobby and it had glass doors which were closed. Inside the reception room there was a group of my peers playing cards. I began crawling on the floor so that they would not see me. I noticed that my friend was in the lobby but just stood there silently, as though she wanted to give me some silent support. She then walked up to me and told me that she thought I should change jobs and that I would never be happy in my current position.

My crawling around the floor in the dream was, of course, very symbolic of the position which I was in—one of struggle. The blocked parking lot represented my career path. The scene of my peers playing a card game was an excellent representation of *Corporate Cult* politics. In another dream a few nights later, I simply dreamed that I was trying to get through a door, which was locked, and I knew that I was the only one who had the key. This, too, represented the roadblocks in my career. This also symbolized my inner truth that only I could save myself or take myself out of the situation. I had to take control of what happened somehow and not look externally for solutions.

These are just a few of the very figurative and descriptive dreams, which I experienced. These dreams allowed my true self to talk to me on a level, which seemed primal. Because I felt blocked and trapped, I was blocked and trapped.

Please don't dismiss your dreams lightly and do record them. Although you can get help in interpreting them, know that there are messages in your dreams, which only you can decipher. Certain associations for you may not allow others to arrive at the same meanings. However, there are many who are truly at a loss when it comes to dream interpretation, so I suggest that if you are in that position, please record them and discuss them with someone you trust; a friend, relative, or a professional. These types of dreams should be regarded as a gift and not as nightmares. I don't mean to imply that every single dream has meaning vital to your life's journey, although it may. I am suggesting that you not simply dismiss dreams about key topics that may be causing you stress. There are many who experience this type of stress, who are incapable of dreaming in such a revealing way.

One man with whom I worked told me that he had a frustrating dream of driving in his car and sitting at a traffic light which would only turn red and yellow. The green light never flashed. He could not move forward. This was a clear sign for him of feeling stopped and in need of caution.

Corporate America has caused the work force to become very defensive and fearful. Based on what workers observe, they may be afraid to accept "constructive" feedback for fear that it is not given in their own best interest to inspire improvement, but as a signal of the beginning of the end. This is a vicious cycle, for fear prohibits employees from listening with open ears and true receptivity and can immediately cause a blocking type of defense. This only allows the cult to point out that the employee is defensive and not open to constructive feedback. Then the cycle becomes a self-fulfilling prophecy.

My dreams changed after I left the *Corporate Cult*. There was a gradual shift. One dream involved me participating in an exam with my work group. The exam was administered by "upper levels" in the department. As I attempted to take the exam I was confronted with one roadblock after another. First my pen would not write, so I used a pencil. The tip broke off and I had no other writing utensils. I asked a peer next to me if I could borrow one and I was reprimanded for talking. I then tried to type my responses to the test questions, only to find that I had no ribbon in my typewriter. I turned on my computer and the familiar program, which I had been using, had been replaced with a new complex version. It was frustrating and I began to shake as I lost my ability to breathe. I decided to walk to the restroom. The walk entailed traveling down a long dark hall and down a long steel staircase. Above the stairs was a sign: *restrooms*. At the bottom of the stairs I found no rooms at all, only a long drop.

When I realized that I was literally at a dead end, I turned to go back up the staircase as I saw a large man in a business suit coming toward me with cold determination. He stood and looked at me awhile, and then informed me that he had been sent to kill me. I begged him to stop and reconsider, but he laughed. Then I changed my strategy and told him I'd do *anything* for him if he would let me live. He agreed and pulled out a twenty dollar bill as payment. Just as I was about to fulfill my end of the bargain, three small children ran down the stairs and surrounded me and the man. I agreed that the deal was off and he could no longer kill me, since he had been exposed by the children. I gave him back a few dollars and went back up the stairs still searching for a restroom down the long dark hall.

The vice president of my department poked his head out of a door and whispered to me, "You know we'll still get you. It's just a matter of time and you'll be dead." I awoke. This dream was so packed with symbols and signs. My inability to complete the exam because I did not have nor could I find appropriate utensils represented my frustration. I was attempting to survive in and transform *Corporate America* without the right tools. The unwillingness of peers to lend me a utensil was a metaphor for the lack of peer support that I experienced.

In the dream, my attempt to find the restroom symbolized release and cleansing, which I was unable to do because there was only a dead end for me; no way out. The man who tried to kill me was a CEO. We seduced each other with "services," until I was rescued by the children. They represented my playful, intuitive, creative force. I still had these gifts when I left corporate life. I felt encouraged. To me this meant that I would be able to further nurture my intuitive and creative side.

In another dream, I was being released as a prisoner of war. I remember having mixed feelings as my master gave me freedom. I was happy to be liberated, yet scared since I had known no other way of life. The master's face got dimmer and dimmer as I awoke from the dream feeling bittersweet. "At least he took care of my basic needs," was the thought on my mind. I felt this way when I left my corporate career behind. There was so much rebirth on the horizon yet "old habits die hard" and my lower self—the victim—mourned her slow, but unavoidable demise.

In one positive dream I was under water. A large friendly female dolphin swam by and asked me to hold onto her. I clasped her friendly flipper and she carried me with her through cool and clear, blue water. The feeling of the dream was so very pleasant and nurturing that I didn't want it to end. I remember feeling disappointed when I awoke. This dream represented a new found freedom and wisdom. It was as though the mysteries of the deep blue sea were to become my own. Being an Aquarian, the water bearer, it seemed so appropriate. The fact that the dolphin was a female and that water itself is yin or female made me feel sure that my creativity was about to grow.

Many people say they don't dream. I believe they do. The dreams simply are not revealed due to defenses or levels of your consciousness. Try to remember them. Tell yourself you will.

Survival and Transformation Strategies

1. Work with your dreams to reveal your authentic self. Use this precious insight from our own creative juices.
   A. Sleep with either a small tape recorder near your pillow or a pen and note pad on your night table.
   B. Interpretation of dreams can lead to remarkable insight into one's deepest intuitive and subconscious needs. By doing this, dream recording is easy and becomes a habit. When you awake in the middle of the night and a dream is fresh, take advantage of this time to somehow store its message. Probably a simple word or phrases will jog your memory. The fact that you take

these notes will assist in bringing the dreams into your conscious mind for analysis the next day.

C. Before you go to sleep at night, take two minutes to tell yourself that you shall remember your dreams and that you will dream about what you need to learn or understand. This can be done with simple affirmations stating, "I will remember my dreams. I will learn what I need to." If for some reason, affirmations are not comfortable for you, you may simply reflect on this thought.

D. When you wake up each morning, take two minutes to scan your mind for dreams. Do this in silence and do it whether or not you believe that you have dreamed. The chances are you have, but may not remember them since the alarm ignites thoughts of your upcoming daily routine.

Personal Journaling

CHAPTER SEVEN
Dis Ease = Disease

We are always stronger when we do not try to fight reality.

Nathaniel Branden

Disease is related to consciousness and self love. This theory is becoming more widely accepted. Bernie Siegel, M.D., Dean Ornish, M.D., and Deepak Chopra, M.D. are a few of the well known doctors who embrace alternative healing.

There are healers like Louise L. Hay and Shatki Gawin who believe that visualization and the connectedness of positive affirmations greatly impact one's state of health and put one into a state of ease.

Companies complain more and more about health care costs and so they should because the costs are rising fiercely; however, why do they think so many of the employees are sick? No matter what the environment is, it is true that there will be some percentage of illness, but if employees enjoyed their work environment more, they could find some satisfaction within their work. I have talked with many employees who have been transferred to various departments and have jumped from company to company. By and large when I ask these individuals what their favorite job was and why, the frequent response of favor involves enjoying the work group in which they were employed, peers and bosses. Interesting work can only be as pleasant as the work group allows. Even uninteresting work gains positive momentum when there is truly a team spirit and a trusting camaraderie.

Disease is surely a word that should be taken literally, dis-ease. Illness after illness entered my life throughout my corporate career and the career preparatory period, and graduate school. During my first semester of graduate school at the age of 21, I developed chronic strep throat. I was always tired and in pain. I was so drained that I could barely get out of bed. I just remember sleeping, studying, and drifting through motions. That fall I was put on a very strong antibiotic that caused uncomfortable side effects, for which I had to take other medications. The week after finals, around Christmas, I flew home to get my tonsils out.

I had a very speedy recovery and a few normal weeks of feeling good until I came down with terrible allergies and asthma. The asthma was debilitating for me. I had to set my alarm about thirty minutes early, because it would take me that long to get out of bed in the morning. Just getting my breath was a big hurdle.

We just do not realize how much we take our simplest of bodily functions for granted. Asthma is a particularly frustrating condition, for an asthmatic often looks healthy and normal, yet there is great pain and suffering going on inside the body. Asthmatics are actually deprived of the life source, the life energy, breath itself, which keeps us alive. Many holistic doctors and healers believe that the disease of asthma represents not being able to take in life, feeling smothered, and suppressing feeling or experience. I believe, in fact I know, that this is true.

Stress manifests itself in many different disguises. We need to be able to listen to our body. The quick fix often just moves the illness to another form or body part. This is like treating symptoms and not the cause. I believe that my tonsils being removed may have stopped my sore throat and strep throat, but did not cure the dis-ease, from which I suffered; stress. I was not managing it. It was managing me.

My asthma got worse and worse as I left school and became a corporate employee. People began treating me differently. I am not sure whether they thought I was helpless, and at times I was, or if they perhaps thought it was just an act. This is a perfect illustration of the stress syndrome and how masterfully, yet subtly debilitating it is. The more stress I had, the more dis-ease I had; the less stress reducing activities I was able to do (petting an animal or exercising), so the more stress I had in reaction to my stress reactions!

Approximately a year after I "joined" *Corporate America*, I attended a cousin's wedding on a rainy October day. My asthma was so bad I nearly passed out. I met a woman there who urged me to go to an allergist and explained to me the dangers of asthma. I took her advice and upon my return home immediately made an appointment with an allergist who came highly recommended. After being examined, I was told that I was allergic to a terribly long list of items, which included many animals, mold, dust, ragweed, pollen, and several foods. After looking at the list, I said to myself, "But how can anyone live who is allergic to all of those items?"

Luckily, my allergy doctor had warmth and was very nurturing. He and his very competent staff helped me through some very hard times and treated me for about eight years. What I especially liked about him was that he implied that allergies were not in and of themselves the problem. He frequently asked me about my job and encouraged me to seek other career options. He saw stress as the trigger to many of my breathing problems. I began shots and had a collection of prescriptions. I got the shots as frequently as once a week for a few years until I tapered back to once every three weeks. There were initially two shots, one in each arm, and then I expressed the desire to be able to tolerate animals so he included an extra shot for cats upon my request.

During this treatment I got better but never cured. My symptoms seemed to sporadically go up and down with weather conditions and work conditions. I believed that allergies and asthma were a weakness in my system only brought out in stressful conditions. They also represented the toxins (negative messages) in my body caused by my denials.

I feel that for many years my asthma protected me. It forced me to sleep a lot, which was good as a replenishing process, and provided me with a valid excuse for my non-participation on softball leagues and the like. There was not much anyone could say about the asthma even though I received many sneers from my superiors.

My career choice also gave me another condition, lodged in my stomach. The symptoms were acute pain and indigestion.

After several barium tests and G.I.s, I was prescribed two different types of ulcer medications, along with a variety of other prescriptions, which were for specific symptoms. When doctors would question the stress in my life, I just laughed.

Stress, I thought, is a condition of life and I could not even imagine taking off or putting aside the corporate handcuffs— those bonding me to the *Corporate Cult* and my dis-ease. I was an achiever and there was no way that stress was going to get the best of me. At least not while I was alive! At times I questioned how long that might be.

I remember being so geared toward productivity, that although I began exercising daily, I refused to exercise for the sake of exercise. I would combine it with another activity like walking or jogging to the drug store to pick up an item or to the post office to purchase stamps. At the time I was so rigid in my need to be productive and work oriented that I would never take a bike ride unless it involved doing errands. I did not allow myself fun time to simply release and relax. I felt that during my conscious hours, I needed to be "productive." I see now that because I was so overly occupied with my productivity, I was rarely conscious, at least not in a holistic sense.

I came down with countless colds, fevers, and viruses, which befriended me during my time with the cult. One day I broke out in hives all over my body. Previously I had experienced hives many times in my life, but never like this. I had hives which covered every inch of body . . . but I felt fine, at least I thought I did. I rushed to the allergy doctor and we discovered that I had not done anything different or unusual, which would bring on such a condition. He suggested that I get some bed rest for a few weeks, or even longer.

This was something I would have never considered. My employer was so stringent regarding attendance that I remember going to work with fevers and colds without hesitation.

Now, I think that this is senseless because it only spreads germs to the rest of the work force. However, the company allowed for no sick days and if you took one, it was quite noteworthy and some bosses refused to grant them. They *strongly encouraged* employees to take vacation. Of course, they really couldn't "force you," but you were warned that sick days would reflect upon performance and possibly imply a lack of job commitment.

When my boss saw the hives, which looked like a reptile coat, he sent me home and told me not to come back until they cleared up, as though I had willed them to appear just to spite him. Maybe I did. Maybe the reptile coat represented a new skin, a deeper position in the cult. My secretary tried to convince me that they were stress related and now I see that they clearly were. I think that my boss was truly angry to see the hives and threatened by them because he knew, deep within, that he had contributed to this condition which manifested itself in sheer ugliness. As bad as they looked, they had no feeling, just like the *Corporate Cult*.

These dis-ease warning signals continued to linger in a variety of illnesses and symptoms. They finally left, when I left the situation, the job, and began nurturing myself. A great doctor, who employs the use of acupuncture, polarity testing, pulse diagnosis, homeopathic remedies and auricular medicine, helped me regain my balance and ease.

Careers can be addictive and so can certain work groups. I was placed in the worst of work environments without protecting myself. Although the *Corporate Cult* was quite a seductress, I did voluntarily assume a victim and caretaker position in my interactions with the cult and its players. Many of my friends disagree and tell me that I really had no other choice. This is partially true. I had no control over anything but self. I waited too long to find the ease. I waited too long before I turned in the handcuffs.

In order to have a life of ease, one must first become conscious of any existing dis-ease. There are two words that best describe what we can do to live a life of ease. My point is awareness and only through awareness can we greet balance and moderation.

Many of us continue to eat long after our stomachs are satisfied and full. Many of our pets, domesticated animals, have learned this behavior from us. They lose some of their consciousness or instinct from being caged in a house, just as we lose our instincts through the golden handcuffs. It is more difficult to find an overfed wild animal. In the past, I've fed squirrels, chipmunks and other furry friends daily in my yard and watch them leave food behind when they are full. They are not obsessed with cleaning their plates. Now I realize they need only nature's food and should not be fed by people.

If we wish to grow in consciousness and be dis-ease free, we need to become more aware and more conscious of what we are doing to our bodies.

Becoming Aware

I have listed a few conservative activities designed to enhance awareness and raise consciousness which take little extra time or effort out of your schedule, only enough to decide to do them.

1. **Choose five products or as many as you can, to which you are very brand loyal and use on a regular basis.** Go out and purchase competitive products in each of these categories. Try to select products that you have never tried before. Try an environmentally safe product! This simple exercise will open your mind up to new ideas and it will help you broaden your perspective. It is small, but it is definitely a start. Your mind will automatically begin assessing and comparing the products as you use them and you will be able to begin evaluating each one, determining what you like and do not like about them. This exercise works better if you choose to replace products you've used for a long time. You can always go back to your original brand if you so desire. But at least take the opportunity to make a change. Try to use the entire portion of the new product and do not toss it out before it is depleted. The product could be shaving cream, toothpaste, soap, hair spray, mustard, yogurt, cologne, juice or any variety of others.

2. **Go out and see five movies, preferably within one month, the more stimulating the better.** For some, this is easy and not a big thing, but for many, it is an eye opening experience. Try to select dramas as well as comedies. Choose films that deal with serious topics, controversy or perhaps political views. If at all possible, include two foreign movies as two out of the five that you see. You may decide to rent them. Sometimes we have a tendency to see movies about people just like us, living in our lifestyle and that just keeps us

separate from the rest of the world. It does not open and expand our reality and does not nurture our highest consciousness to the maximum.

3. **Go out and do something you have never done before.** Try to select an activity in which you are interested. Some may require lessons or instruction, while others may only require the time investment. The activity does not need to take up a great deal of time. Here are some suggestions are: bowling, ice skating, roller skating, playing tennis, ping-pong, riding a bicycle built for two, sketching, paint a watercolor, sewing, cooking a dish you have never attempted, golfing, horseback riding, water skiing, salsa dancing or whatever you desire.

4. **Sit down and write two letters.** These letters can be to your parents, siblings, cousins, college friends, grandparents, or whomever. I want to clarify that I am not speaking of notes or sending cards. Write a letter a few pages long to familiarize yourself with your own thoughts and feelings. You will be surprised at the realizations that you will make once you decide to do this mental expression. This is a strong step toward nurturing your intuition. It is especially helpful to choose someone to write to whom you trust a great deal, someone with whom you feel comfortable being real. I want to clarify that these are not to be business letters.

5. **Attend a lecture and/or a documentary.** Many communities hold such programs free of charge or at a minimal cost at local libraries, art museums, or universities. Check with the cultural centers in your area. These programs will provide

your mind with a new stimulus, and help to broaden your perspective. The closer you are to seeing things in a worldly fashion or more global viewpoint, the chances are higher that your consciousness shall be slowly raised. Topics in this area may include the Holocaust, slavery, the environment, AIDS, book reviews covering autobiographies, animals, self-help, fiction, philosophy, religion, history, fitness and diet. Challenge yourself by selecting topics, which you know very little about or perhaps don't care about. You may be surprised.

6. **Go to your local library and spend one or two hours at the magazine section reviewing magazines that you have never read or heard of.** If you prefer, pick up a few new ones at the newsstand. This will not, however, be as effective as attending the library, where the choices are almost without limit.

   While you are at the library, do the same with books. Peruse the library in full and look at the new book section. Scan books that are alarming or even absurd. Select topics which do compliment your job or education. See the bigger picture and find another perspective.

Some of these tasks can be done on the internet. I would also encourage trying activities that you have not attempted since childhood, whether it be jacks or going to the zoo. Remember that the object is not to like all these new activities, but to experience them and to then do some self-analysis about how they felt for you. Did they produce or help you to release tension and why? Keep some notes on what happened and you will slowly learn more about your psychic awareness of the universe. You will also realize that the world is a big place and your problems and stresses will seem less threatening.

Survival and Transformation Strategies

1. **Define your dis-ease.** Make a list of the individuals in your work environment who you believe contribute to your dis-ease. Next, write down what possible impact they have on your career, how they are viewed by your peers, their peers, their boss, and themselves—to the best of your knowledge. Go by your hunches. Then note the specific behaviors that you find offensive, maybe they just make you uncomfortable. Go through each behavior and decide how you can more effectively accept it. This may take confrontation, patience, letting go and detachment or you may decide to join a support group or seek psychological counsel. It amazes me that in many circles, even today, counseling is regarded as being for those who are weak or flawed. This is part of the cult mentality that prevents people from getting the support they may need.

   There are also community groups available to provide support for those of us who work with "rage-aholics," alcoholics, or other specific types of dysfunctional individuals. I encourage you to seek them out. Go for yourself and experience the growth and support you deserve.

2. **Assess yourself emotionally, physically, intellectually and spiritually.** These are the four areas needing balance in the human psyche in many ancient cultures. They are represented

in the medicine wheel by the four directions: The south represents the physical, the west is the emotional and intuitive, the north is spiritual, and the east is intellectual. Take a look at where you are in these areas and where you want to be. What are you willing to give up to get to where you want to go? I believe that you can only "have it all" if your expectations are realistic and not greedy. A truly wealthy man is able to say when he has enough.

3. **Maximize your accomplishments. Don't minimize your accomplishments.** Maximize them. Celebrate your successes; all of them! I'm not suggesting boasting, just personal satisfaction and self-honor. Send yourself positive messages, letters and emails. Use voice mail to leave yourself a positive and loving message. It may be the only one you hear that day. Be your own cheerleader, not your own worst enemy, a role many of us assume.

4. **Develop a support system.** Whether we want to believe it or not, we all need a support system. The bigger the better. Find ways in which you feel comfortable getting support and surround yourself with supportive people. Your support list could include: family, friends, church groups, hobby organizations, clubs, pets (yes, pets) and actual support groups. You will find that when you begin looking for support groups, you will find many out there.

Personal Journaling

CHAPTER EIGHT
The System Rules

I came across the following eight "System Rules" and decided that they match the unstated rules in the secret book of the *Corporate Cult*:

1. **Control.** Be in control of all behavior and interaction.

2. **Perfection.** Always be "right."

3. **Blame.** If something doesn't happen as you planned, blame yourself, or someone else.

4. **Denial.** Any feelings are denied, especially one's life anxiety.

5. **Unreliability.** People are not to be counted on.

6. **Incompleteness.** Don't bring transactions to completion or resolution. Keep others off track.

7. **No Talk.** Don't talk openly and directly. Be secretive.

8. **Disqualification.** When disrespectful, shameful, abusive or compulsive behaviors occur, disqualify it, deny it, or disguise it.

These System Rules are, in fact, from the book *Facing Shame: Families in Recovery*, by Merle Fossom and Marialy Mason and they are meant to describe family rules of shame-bound systems. The coincidence that they also describe the rules of the *Corporate Cult* is not surprising. Virginia Satir, John Bradshaw and many others estimate that the percentage of the U.S. population in dysfunctional families is about 96-97 percent. Dysfunction can be caused by a number of traumas, disorders and life situations. Dysfunction manifests itself in substance abuse, most commonly observed as drugs and alcohol; and most commonly ignored as food, workaholism, chain smoking, and countless other more secretive compulsive behaviors.

Corporate America, and indeed, society, is made up of these dysfunctional families. Healing and transforming an entire system of such magnitude is not possible, at least not today. One can, however, transform one's own viewpoint and have a full career by lifting the veils of ignorance and acknowledging these truths. Dysfunctional systems do not foster self-esteem, in fact, they diminish confidence and foster fear and anger. By forcing the control issue, the system sets up the parameters for the dictatorship.

Here is an example of a boss wanting complete control. In this case, the need for control clearly went too far. A middle manager employee had announced that she would be going on a diet to drop a few pounds. She ordered her employee to go to lunch with her so that they could discuss business. The employee informed her boss that she would attend the lunch meeting but would probably not eat since she had planned to skip lunch each day in order to lose weight. Her boss, a female, aggressively and abrasively informed her that she would go and she "would indeed eat because it was to be a 'bonding experience.'"

The elusive standard of perfection is another control tool. It immediately puts everyone into "their place" and humiliates them. The humiliation and shame caused by the realization that one is not perfect leads to blaming the boss or subordinate who is more "less perfect" than the one blaming, or so one would like to think. In the system, since one is always vulnerable to blame, one cannot trust anyone in the system. These harsh feelings are just too painful to impose on one's self or on the very system which pays the household bills, so we deny it all.

By denying these unrealistic rules which are silently agreed upon during cult initiation, we become incomplete and dishonest about what is really happening and our feelings are disguised. What is "supposed to happen," as though we were in a play, becomes far more seemingly real and important than what is actually going on.

An effective way to cement group cohesiveness is to ferment the group's hatred of an external enemy. Deficiencies within the group can be easily and painlessly overlooked by focusing attention on the deficiencies or "sins" of the cult.

They consider each other the enemy and not the solution to the problems of manpower and earning a living. The work force, in many instances, has resorted to fierce internal competition in place of cooperation. The latter is conducive to high self-esteem and competence. The former takes root with the dysfunction of the *Corporate Cult* ideals.

Unfortunately, the tone of *Corporate America* has made competition inside a corporation, among peers, to be a threatening focus of our work force.

There are many variables that impact our relationships and *Corporate Cult*ure. Some are:

- power struggles,
- playing favorites,
- the facade of teamwork,
- lack of flow,
- communication disconnects,
- insufficient, or the lack of, recognition,
- a climate of suspicion and intimidation,
- dismissal of employees' suggestions without full consideration or for poorly defined reasons,
- turf conflicts,
- a lack of conscious caring for fellow coworkers, combined with organizational needs,
- jealousy and envy.

These variables are owned and guarded by the *Corporate Cult*. Rosabeth Moss Kanter says that internal competition is bad because: players end up paying more attention to beating their rivals than to performing the task well; friendly competitiveness among people who respect one another turns into mistrust, suspicion and scorn; imitation begins to drive out innovation; the weaker party may give up rather than continue to fight to the detriment of the company; and, the stronger party begins to feel dangerously invincible.

These are lessons that *Corporate America* and its employees have chosen to learn the hard way. The basic ethical premises which counter this strategy of internal demise have been around since our ancient cultures. Aristotle, Laotse, Rumi and countless others have given us ethical principles and philosophies.

Survival and Transformation Strategies

1. **Reassess your personal boundaries.** By boundaries I do not mean your office size. I'm speaking of your mental boundaries; the parameters of your "self." How closely do you allow people to get to you? Do you let people get in too close? Do you share too much of business with other people? Are you the other extreme with boundaries as high as a fort? Are your boundaries so high and thick that they prohibit you from enjoying others?

2. **Know the role you play in or with your work group.** Consider your formal and informal roles. Be honest with yourself and decide if this is a position that you want to keep. Does it make you feel good about yourself? Why? Why not? Does it coincide with your view of self?

3. **Be cautious about time management advice and time management classes.** So many time management classes encourage balancing several balls at once. If you are not careful, you may complicate and add chaos to your life by driving to an appointment in rush hour, while trying to talk

on your car phone and use your portable tape recorder. The goal is peace, not turmoil. Manage your time carefully and selfishly. It is all that you have in this life and it carries us through life so very quickly. Savor special and sacred moments. Someone once told me that you could tell how healthy you are by what you do with the gift of leisure time. Make a healthy choice, not a cluttered one. Don't do many things at once. Do one thing at a time and do it well, then rest and replenish. Nurture and honor yourself. Never worship your tasks.

4. **Nurture your intuition.** There are so many things one can do to develop intuitive ability:

   A. First you must relax. Relaxation can heal and clear the mind, it heals with comfort. "Relaxing" means different things to different people and in our manic society, it has become an art. Some common prescriptions of relaxing are:

      - quietly listening to music
      - quietly sitting in front of a fire
      - sitting at pool side
      - curling up with a novel
      - spending quiet time with loved ones or your pet
      - taking a leisurely walk
      - playing golf
      - watching television

   Schedule daily relaxation time. If this is simply not possible, then I suggest that it be done weekly.

Relaxation time should optimally be time spent alone while participating in very minimal activity in near silence. The average person cannot clear the mind very easily if there is a physical activity, interaction, or "noise" input occurring. You will find that when your mind is clear, you will receive new ideas, insights, and understandings. You will also build your resolve.

During this period, it is very important to practice deep breathing. This is also an excellent tool to practice at the office before, during, and after high stress episodes. Be sure that you feel your abdomen lift and expand as it fills with breath, your life force. So often we are too "stressed out" to breathe and this undermines our ability to function optimally. Breathe and be aware of your breath, feel it. One has to take life in, in order to let it out or let it go. By not breathing in, we do not take in or experience situations. By not breathing in, we cannot exhale. Embrace each breath and then let it go. Embrace fear and then let it go. Embrace your anger and then let it go. Embrace your happiness, experience it and then let it go so that life can bring you NEW BREATH, A NEW LESSON, A NEW HEIGHT.

B. I encourage meditation. There are many different types. Meditation is simple and has no cost. One may sit quietly and focus on the breath for a given amount of time, usually twenty minutes, in order to gain full benefits. Many communities have access to classes on meditation and relaxation for those who want to learn more. Although meditation does develop intuition, it is a fabulous stress reducer and can calm the blood pressure and heart.

For those willing to take the next step, I suggest visualization. This is another inexpensive and easy technique. It can be adjusted to work for you and your specific stresses.

First, get into a relaxed and comfortable state. Then imagine a stressful situation at work. See the situation in your mind's eye. Take the time to notice the clothes that people are wearing and see the setting. Take in the sounds. Now play the situation out in your mind, exactly as you wish it to occur with the most desirable outcome. See yourself winning and handling the situation. See everyone being pleased with the outcome.

Only work with positives! Take a few moments each morning and/or evening to do this. Use different situations if you desire. If something has already happened that has you very stressed, then imagine yourself happily finding the right solutions to ease your stress. The more detail in your visualization, the better it shall work for you.

You may want to take a slow deep breath and blow the situation out of your mouth into a pink crystal ball, letting it loose into the universe. Cleanse your body of the stress. Use as many sounds and colors as your imagination can create. If you have a difficult time with the details, don't worry. I have worked with many people in this area and the improvement comes swiftly with consistency. After just a week of doing this, there is usually noticeable improvement in one's attitude, sense of control, confidence, and peace of mind.

C. Use affirmations. Affirmations are one of the most powerful tools that we can use. Those who are very devoted to raising their corporate consciousness and self esteem work with affirmations in many ways. Affirmations are statements which create and reinforce a positive self image and confidence level.

When working with affirmations, it is most effective to use your name in each statement. For example, someone who works in the *Corporate Cult* environment may work with the following affirmations:

- I, [your name], am an excellent employee.

- I, [your name], respect myself and my work. My coworkers notice this and respect me as well.

- I, [your name], work with dignity and, therefore, I only allow others to approach me with dignity. In turn, I, [your name], respect others and approach them with dignity.

- I, [your name], am a peaceful and fair person and I take time to relax.

These affirmations need to be read or written daily. They can easily be affixed to a bathroom mirror. Read them first thing in the morning and at night before bed.

You may also want to make a cassette tape, in your own voice, of affirmations. This is especially powerful. You can listen to it in the car or while falling asleep.

Make sure the affirmations are all positive toward yourself and others. Avoid using negative words. For example, instead of saying, "I, Karen, am not treated unfairly," say "I, Karen, am treated fairly. I expect fair treatment and I am always fair with others."

D. Exercise is becoming an American cliché. You don't have to join a club. A brisk walk or a stationary bike can help, too. Don't exclude exercise as an option.

The chances are that if you are in a high stress position, you come home late and with very little energy. Start off slowly—twice a week. See how you feel afterwards. You may decide to increase your time. You can incorporate it into an activity with your friends, spouse or family, so that you won't be deprived of time with your support system.

A well-balanced nutritious eating program will only help you raise your self-esteem and awareness. We put so many preservatives and pollutants into our systems daily, it is no wonder that we can't handle the stress. We stress our own systems with poor diets. Find a healthy eating program that works for your taste and body. Incorporate as much natural fresh food as possible and, of course, lots of water. By providing your body with the nutrients and energy it needs, you'll be surprised what it can do for you.

- Counseling and support groups. This option still remains stigmatized, even today. Although these methods are certainly not for everyone, they work effectively for many. Don't rule them out as options.

Depending on your situation, they may be the first place that you should turn.

- Holistic resources. There are a group of supportive resources that I will call holistic because they improve health and well being. Some resources to which I am referring are Yoga, Tai Chi, and Feldenkrais. These movement patterns fine-tune the body by gently improving flexibility, circulation, coordination, posture and breathing. They are all very relaxing and inexpensive to practice.

Personal Journaling

CHAPTER NINE
How Did the Corporate Cult Get Its Power?

The blue mountain ... the white cloud. They are quite independent, but yet dependent. This is how we live, and how we practice zazen.

Tozan, *Zen Mind, Beginner's Mind*

The *Corporate Cult* is sterile. People are programmed to not feel. The handshake doesn't mean what it used to. There is often little honor and few ethics passing between many who make exchanges in the corporate environment. The myth says that it is about the good of the whole and the good of the team. Everyone pretends to believe these empty statements, while following their own private agenda. When I think of handshakes, I think of the night before my wedding when we had the rehearsal. It took place in a Catholic Church and I witnessed the priest telling my fiancé and father to shake hands before my father "handed me over to him." I was appalled. I felt insulted and uncomfortable as they stood shaking hands in front of me, as though I were a commodity, some business deal. I am sure that many people didn't, but it was just too symbolic of the *Corporate Cult* for me so I stopped the rehearsal and insisted on a change. We agreed after a brief discussion that my father and my fiancé would embrace instead of shake hands, which made me feel very happy and comfortable. After all, it was a ceremony about love, not business.

Sometimes I wonder if the American society has lost most passion. In so many ways each day we become more and more void of this marvelous and mystical energy which keeps life going. To me, the handshake and embrace are a metaphor. I want to embrace life, not shake on it. I understand that handshaking, for a number of reasons works in a business setting and I am *not* advocating business hugs. I am advocating that we employ flexibility and true people skills wherever possible and in all interactions.

Who Is America

Just as the victims of the Holocaust pass down their sadness and grief to the younger generation, we all pass down our experiences. In America we have a population made up of immigrants. Let's face it, unless you are a Native American, one of your ancestors came here from another place. That has many ramifications. Some immigrants came with a strong desire. Others were forced to come here. Considering the major move and sacrifices encountered by immigrants it is likely that some needs were not met. The Depression also caused many to feel a struggle to survive. Was there struggle? Who was left behind? What needs were not met? When basic needs were not met, voids existed and these voids sometimes turned into neuroses, deep seated fears or hysteria which have most likely been passed on through various generations.

The movie, *Pele, the Conqueror*, does an exquisite job of demonstrating the bravery and strength which it took for many people to migrate here. If you have ever moved, even within the same city, you know that this can be traumatic and ranks very high on the stress scale. Imagine moving to another country, leaving behind friends, family, identity, customs, land and maybe all of your possessions. I believe that this crisis which so many of our ancestors have experienced still lives within our families and deeply within our cells.

This is one of the reasons that the *Corporate Cult* exists today. These ancestors experienced loss and it was too painful. They found ways to feel less and have taught these ways to their children, as an effective survival technique. The business community built *Corporate Cults* with those of us who were programmed to feel less and accept corporate abuse in order to survive financially, without a monetary struggle. The trade-off seemed worth it: Take a little abuse and be awarded the "golden handcuffs." The problem is, of course, that there is really little and often *no* true monitoring of such abuse. We need to monitor it for ourselves through the building of strong and healthy self-esteem. If we allow it, the *Corporate Cult* fosters and nurtures the dysfunction that we learned in unhealthy family settings.

Many immigrants came from countries in which people had very transparent physical and psychological boundaries. These boundaries were dictated by the customs of each individual land. It was much more difficult to develop strong boundaries in places where several people lived in one small dwelling, or had to use public baths, or simply had little privacy in their experience. This lack of privacy and boundary building intermeshed people in such a way that they sometimes experienced shame and a lack of dignity. This was true also for many of those who came to this country by sea routes. Everyone was "packed in."

In some cases, this pendulum has swung the other way and many survivors of these situations need and honor a great deal of physical and emotional boundaries. Could it be possible that this phenomenon is particularly responsible for the impersonal and cold shouldered parts of the country. We hear about people not being as friendly in places like New York City. It is a lot easier to be neighborly in the Midwest, where you can go back into your suburban home with a defined lot, maybe a fence. In suburbia, one generally experiences minimal risks through demonstrating neighborly behavior because one has strong physical boundaries of space and protection. In the city it is easy to get into someone else's space; in fact, it is quite difficult to get out of somebody else's space.

I lived in New York City for a while and I remember coming home to an apartment after a rather pleasant day in which I did very little physical or mental work, but still felt entirely exhausted. This was from the interference of boundaries and energies which, in the city, constantly invade space. If one was neighborly in such a place, it could result in danger on a physical, psychological, and emotional level.

The Civil War and The Melting Pot

Our country by its very nature consists of people from all lands. There will always be different values, religions, opinions, and perspectives. Yet as humans we unconsciously aim for oneness and unity. Unity implies we are conscious; a kindred spirit of acceptance and understanding exists among all creatures. However, to an unconscious mind it means that everyone should be the same and agree. There is such great diversity in this country and it has so many voices echoing from several groups. This began as early as the Civil War when our country was so young and growing. Many believe that the Civil War has been over for years and years but in fact it lives on each and every day within neighborhoods, Congressional Hearings and, I gravely point out, even in churches.

In the name of God, we continue to judge people and repress certain ethnic groups. Spike Lee's *Do The Right Thing* was fundamentally a movie about the Civil War. The new manifestation calls itself racial tension and discrimination, but isn't it just another form of psychological slavery?

Understand that the friction is not necessarily a bad thing. Of course, a nonviolent friction would be ideal. Without the friction, there is no chance of winning and resolution. Diversity exists in *Corporate America* and it acts out the fundamentals of the Civil War each and every day in the work place. Corporate energy is often focused on changing the differences instead of integrating strengths held by each group into the collective group.

I frequently find myself in group situations which make me feel very uncomfortable. For a long time I couldn't pinpoint the exact cause. After examining this feeling, the dynamics, and characteristics of these particular groups, I have come to notice that these group situations are homogenous. I look around and I see groups of white people with the same income level, same education level, the same interests, driving the same automobiles, and they probably have their kids in the same day care centers. I get a feeling from these types of situations that scares me deeply. Too many like-minded people can only see in one direction. This is why diversity is so important and a major key to creativity and growth. I know that I am especially sensitive to this issue because of my upbringing in integrated situations.

I remember my first few days at graduate school. I kept wondering where "the rest" of the students were. Where were the minority students? Those I saw all looked alike. I felt so out of place, as though someone had just created me with a cookie cutter. I was created that way with thousands of other students from the same mold. Although I fit in demographically, in many ways I felt a resistance on a larger scale.

It was uncomfortable for me to be with such a large group of the same kind of people. I had never experienced this before. I remember telling fellow students that the environment was an unusual one for me because there was little integration. I explained that my high school was about 40 percent black as was the undergraduate college that I attended. In addition, my classmates were from all socioeconomic walks of life. Some had parents on welfare and others had parents who had Ph.D.s. I often hear, "there were black people in my high school too; I had one in my history class and we even ate lunch with him sometimes."

By *being aware* of the behaviors and philosophical differences of the world, we become more conscious. Consciousness is the key to life.

The clearer our insight into what is beyond good and evil, the more we can embody the good.

Tao Te Ching

As referred to in a previous chapter, today, concepts like emotional IQ and mind viruses or memes are becoming the new concepts of the workplace. They help our consciousness.

Survival and Transformation Strategies

1. **If you are not sure whether you like your job, ask yourself if you would wish your current employment situation on your son, daughter, or a close friend.** This may help you weed through some denial and repressed awareness.

2. **Accept the fact that the company is paying you to do certain things and to behave in certain ways, from dressing to dining.** If you cannot accept this peacefully, you probably need to do extra relaxation or stress releasing activities or find another job with fewer personal demands. If you have a strong identity, you may be just what the *Corporate Cult* needs to challenge their system. If you decide to challenge the system, do it gently, firmly, and as a dignified adult.

    Any other behavior will leave you wide open for ridicule and self-sabotage.

3. **Always realize that you are replaceable and that there will always be someone more capable, or at least someone who is perceived as being more capable than you.** Don't overestimate your worth to the cult. The esteemed cult

167

characteristics are selfishness, greed, and conformity. Therefore, you can always be cut out. Never underestimate your self worth and your worth to your family. To thy own self be true.

4. **Take a look at your ethnic background with a sociologist's eye.** Many Americans say that they are simply American and that is great. I am patriotic, too. However, look deeply past your American heritage and investigate your ethnicity. Do not deny this wealthy pool of knowledge. Here you will visit your deepest strengths and weaknesses, which have been handed down subtly and subliminally in many cases. Don't run from them. Greet them with open arms. Understand them.

Personal Journaling

CLOSING THOUGHTS

Recently I interviewed at a college for a faculty position. After the interview, the interviewer, a former corporate businessman, winked at me. I wanted to say, "Oh, do you need a tissue? Have you something in your eye?"

Instead I smiled very *coolly* and closed the door, realizing that one can never leave the *Corporate Cult* behind in the physical sense. One can leave the *Corporate Cult* behind through the methods of detachment, *internal focus,* a strong sense of self and a healthy support system. Just because your boss is a member of the *Corporate Cult*, you don't have to join. You can survive and transform, quit, or join the cult.

If you can respect your boss, that is really all for which you can ask. If you like and respect your boss, you are extremely fortunate. If you do not, you can be sure that some of the cult dynamics are in your career.

Playing the victim is like skating uphill. You will only find yourself at the mercy of the *Corporate Cult*. Don't be overly intimidated to rock the boat, they may throw you overboard anyway.

Is *Corporate America* as awful as I make it out to be? In spots, absolutely. Are there a lot of great dynamics happening in *Corporate America* that bond healthy business dealings and encourage growth, respect and creativity? In spots, absolutely.

To Laugh Often

To laugh often and much; to win the respect of intelligent people and the affection of children; to earn the appreciation of honest critics and endure the betrayal of false friends; to appreciate beauty; to find the best in others; to leave the world a bit better whether by a healthy child, a garden patch, or a redeemed social condition; to know even one life has breathed easier because you lived. This is to have succeeded.

Ralph Waldo Emerson

Good Luck.

Transformation and Survival Strategies

1. Employ humor into your life.

2. Try to be more flexible, open-minded and accepting with others.

3. Accept that performance does not always matter.

4. Don't allow yourself to be bullied at work, even by your boss.

5. Ask for feedback on your performance.

6. Don't allow anger or any negative emotion to immobilize you.

7. Gain focus on yourself.

8. Feed yourself positive talk.

9. Have a plan.

10. Realize that your reality is just that—your reality.

11. Don't believe that merely because something isn't just, it won't happen.

12. Ask yourself what your job does for you and write down the answers on a sheet of paper.

13. Don't take "it" personally, whatever "it" may be.

14. Don't rely on employment law to protect you.

15. Be aware of your emotional IQ and try to strengthen it with keen awareness of yourself and others.

16. Get out of the *think* and examine what memes you might have that are holding you back on the job, and in life.

17. Explore your shadows.

18. Get an attorney.

19. Document your career and keep the document in a safe place.

20. Don't depend on logic to help you survive.

21. Work with your dreams to reveal your authentic self.

22. Define your dis-ease.

23. Assess yourself emotionally, physically, intellectually and spiritually.

24. Maximize your accomplishments.

25. Develop a support system.

26. Reassess your personal boundaries.

27. Know the role you play in or with your work group.

28. Be cautious of time management advice and time management classes.

29. Nurture your intuition.

30. If you are not sure whether you like your job, ask yourself if you would wish your current employment situation on your son, daughter, or close friend.

31. Accept the fact that the company is paying you to do certain things and to behave in certain ways, from dressing to dining.

32. Always realize that you are replaceable and that there will always be someone more capable, or at least someone who is perceived as being more capable than you.

33. Take a look at your ethnic background with a sociologist's eye.